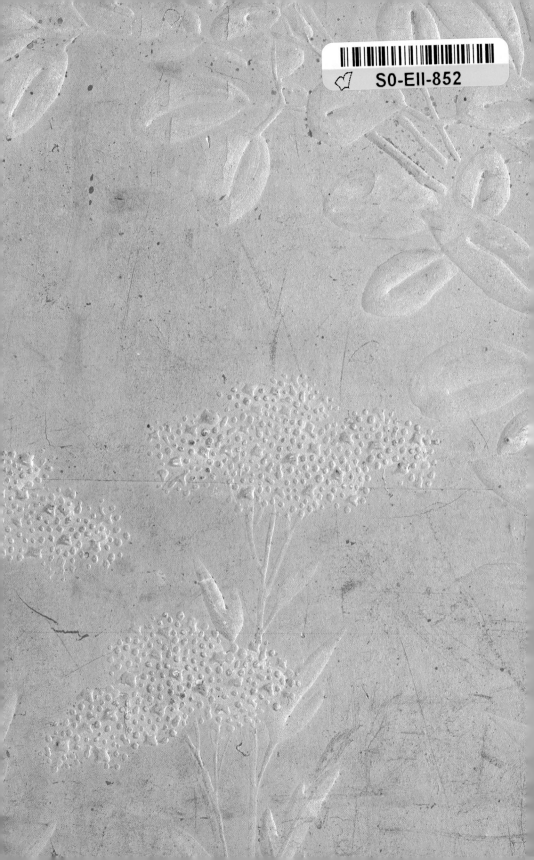
S0-EII-852

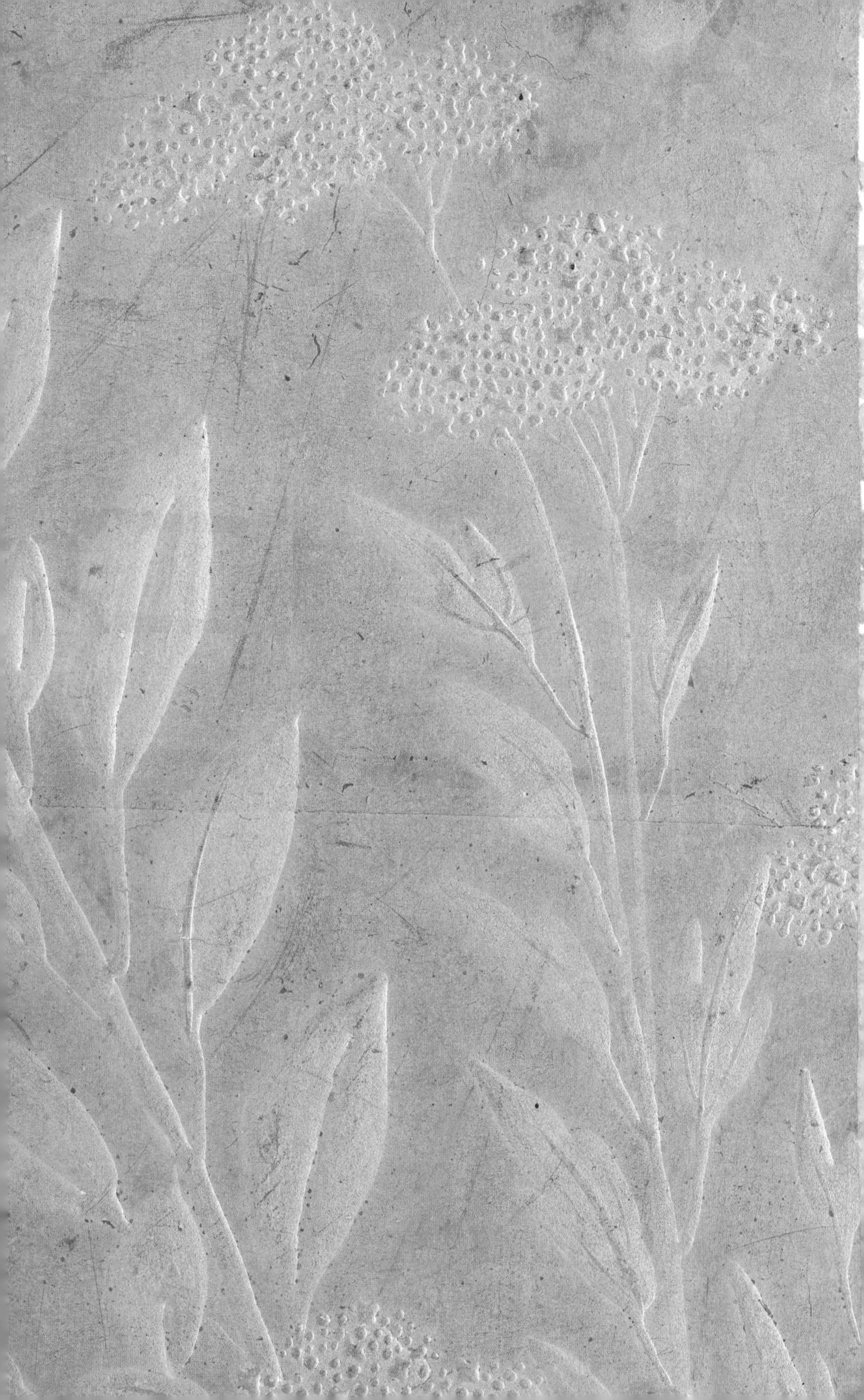

HEAVENLY ORDER

TWENTY FIVE MEDITATIONS OF
WISDOM AND HARMONY

HEAVENLY ORDER

TWENTY FIVE MEDITATIONS OF WISDOM AND HARMONY

ALEXANDRA VILLARD DE BORCHGRAVE

PREFACE BY
JULIAN RABY

FOREWORD BY
JAMES T. ULAK

Glitterati
INCORPORATED

New York, New York

First published in the United States of America in 2008 by

Glitterati Incorporated
225 Central Park West
New York, New York 10024
www.GlitteratiIncorporated.com

Copyright © 2008 Alexandra Villard de Borchgrave

All artworks are copyright © Freer Gallery of Art,
Smithsonian Institution as indicated in artwork section of
Heavenly Order.

All rights reserved. No part of this publication may be
reproduced in any form or by any electronic or mechanical
means, including information storage and retrieval systems,
without permission in writing from Glitterati Incorporated,
except by a reviewer who may quote brief passages in a review.

Art Direction and Design: Alexandra Villard de Borchgrave
Mechanical Design: Marta Lapinska
Mechanical Design Layout: Henrique Siblesz
Photography: Neil Greentree/ Freer Gallery of Art

Printed and bound in China by Hong Kong Graphics & Printing Ltd.

10 9 8 7 6 5 4 3 2 1

Library of Congress Cataloging-in-Publication Data

De Borchgrave, Alexandra Villard.
Heavenly order : twenty-five meditations of wisdom and harmony /
Alexandra Villard de Borchgrave ;
preface by Julian Raby ; foreword by James Ulak. -- 1st ed.
   p. cm.
ISBN-13: 978-0-9801557-0-9
I. Title.
PS3604.E123H43 2008
811'.6--dc22

                    2008003462

DEDICATION

To all those who have given

of themselves:

With all the world

in disarray,

One tender blossom

survives;

In the deepest crevasse

of the human soul

The kindness of heart

still thrives.

Alexandra Villard de Borchgrave

CONTENTS

PREFACE
Julian Raby

FOREWORD
James T. Ulak

INTRODUCTION
Alexandra Villard de Borchgrave

 ## BEGINNING
Celestial Design
Heavenly Order

 ## DARKNESS
War
Children of Pain
Kindness of Heart

Waves of Hunger
Leaves of Hope

Chains of Fear
Spirit of Valor

Clouds of Anger
Passion for Fairness

PREFACE

As one of the leading collectors of the Aesthetic Movement, Charles Lang Freer strongly believed in the affective power of the arts, and in beauty as a universal principle. While he is best known for the objects, especially paintings, that he presented to the nation, he was himself an avid reader of romantic poetry. In keeping with Horace's adage *Ut pictura poiesis*, Freer saw the sister arts as combining to heighten sensibility – the Muses in concert conducting the viewer to that moment of vision when he or she becomes lost in the ineffable.

Such aesthetic musings were brought to a standstill by the harsh brutalities of the First World War. While the art world moved in a very different direction, there were other factors of change in the years that followed Freer's death in 1919. The Asian collections of the Freer Gallery expanded, whereas Freer's collection of American art remained – in accord with the dictates of his will – unaltered. This contrast between growth and stasis was accompanied by a burgeoning scholarship that increasingly sought to view Asian art within its native context. The passage of time saw Freer's original vision dimmed. "My greatest desire," he wrote, "has been to unite modern work with masterpieces of certain periods of high civilization harmonious in spiritual suggestion, having the power to broaden aesthetic culture and the grace to elevate the human mind."

In this, her second book of poetry, Alexandra Villard de Borchgrave has once again creatively used images from the collection of the Freer Gallery of Art to accompany her poetry.

In this instance, the images are drawn from Japanese paintings and screens, and she has juxtaposed poetry in a Western idiom with Eastern idioms of painting and calligraphy, bringing together East and West in a manner that recalls Freer's spiritual intentions.

On occasion, the visual image mirrors the verbal – the written "wave" might, for example, find its visible expression in a surging brushstroke on the opposite page. For the most part, though, the references are not express, but allusive, intended to capture a mood or sentiment. Alexandra Villard de Borchgrave has sought to invoke the sister arts of poetry and painting, not one as an illustration of the other, not one in tandem behind the other, but as two simultaneous voices in harmony.

The spirit of this poetry is redemptive, and I trust that Charles Lang Freer would have approved of this book on several levels – the juxtaposition of Western and Eastern traditions, the harmony of arts, and the sentiment of redemption, for as he wrote late in his life, "Art is properly concerned with the living of our lives," and we hold "an instinctive sense that there must be some way through it to reach an understanding that redemption does exist."

JULIAN RABY
Director, Freer Gallery of Art and
Arthur M. Sackler Gallery

FOREWORD

Alexandra Villard de Borchgrave's decision to place the printed text
of her verse over carefully selected images of seventeenth-century
Japanese painting surfaces is inspired. Her diligent research of
the Japanese tradition of linking word and image has produced this
delicate hybrid that invites her readers to imagine a world in which the
dividing line between what is seen and what is said is provocatively fluid.

The Japanese aesthetic Mrs. de Borchgrave has chosen to
reference has a long and complex history but understanding a
few of its basic concepts might enhance the appreciation of this
volume. The foundational element of the Japanese writing system
is the ideogram or kanji. These many thousands of kanji are
beautifully sophisticated abstractions of symbolic drawings. They
form the Japanese "alphabet" of written discourse. In the same
way that handwriting varies with personality, each calligrapher
adds his or her own idiosyncratic touch to the standardized forms
of kanji. In the physical act of inscribing a text, the truly skilled
calligrapher manipulates the ink-charged brush in an interpretive
act, much in the way that a musician handles a score.

The stage for this performance is equally important. Whether
rendered on paper or on silk, the level of absorbency can give the
applied ink a feel of glossy slickness or a sense of cloudy dissipation.
Beyond absorbency, paper can be decorated with a range of
enhancements, including painted images, impressed design patterns,
and collage as well as embossing, dyeing, and the application
of precious metals. When text is inscribed on such surfaces,
the meaning of words can flow into both intended and totally
serendipitous directions.

The long Japanese tradition of placing sacred texts and poetry on very specially prepared surfaces probably evolved from the custom of producing illuminated sutra texts, the sacred Buddhist scriptures. In very short time, this aesthetic was applied to the presentation of secular poetry. Verse inscribed on elaborately prepared surfaces epitomized the aesthetic of Heian period (794-1185) court taste.

At the cusp of the seventeenth century, when power of governance in Japan was solidified unequivocally in the hands of warriors, wider segments of society laid claim to the forms of visual expression that were once the purview of aristocrats. Many of the background images reproduced in this volume show works created in the seventeenth century, which are, in various ways, aspirations to the revival of earlier aesthetic styles.

In an age when words fly in bits and bytes with incredible speed, when tiny devices containing the texts of whole libraries have virtually become appendages to the human body, Alexandra Villard de Borchgrave wisely reminds us of a culture beyond mechanism and utility, one that is grounded in the physical beauty of words.

JAMES T. ULAK
Deputy Director, Freer Gallery of Art and
Arthur M. Sackler Gallery and Curator of Japanese Art

INTRODUCTION

I had not seen the exquisite paintings of the great Japanese artists of the Momoyama period (1573-1615) and the Edo period (1615-1868), most especially the glorious works of Hon'ami Koetsu (1558-1638), that appear in this book when I started writing the poems.

In reflecting on pain, sorrow, love and hope, I searched for a way to give voice to my thoughts about the beauty we have been given in this world and the choices we have made. In a peaceful moment while sitting by the sea, I found that the Ten Worlds of Buddhist philosophy gave me the structure I needed for my work.

The Ten Worlds begin with Hell and end with Buddha, taking us through destructive anger before reaching wisdom and compassion. In each world, there is both the negative and the positive option. Thus, in Hell, we can experience war as well as empathy for others; in Humanity, we can find passivity or laziness and at the same time tranquility; and in Anger, we discover both aggressiveness and a passion to be fair-minded. We end with enlightenment.

I used this structure in a rather loose arrangement, giving my own interpretation to these worlds as I went along. I created a prelude that includes the poems "Celestial Design" and "Heavenly Order," and went on to divide the Ten Worlds into three sections called "Darkness," "Humanity," and "Light."

One day, I called my dear friend and wonderful publisher, Marta Hallett, and read her three of the poems I had written.

Right away she said with her keen insight, "I think seventeenth-century Japanese art, particularly by Hon'ami Koetsu, would be ideal to create a stunning and serene backdrop for your words. I will send you the catalogue of an extraordinary exhibition at the Philadelphia Museum of Art in 2000 of Koetsu's work, so you can see what I mean."

As soon as I received the catalogue, I fell in love with the ethereal quality of Koetsu's masterful renditions of soaring birds and graceful flowers and felt they fit perfectly with my concept of a heavenly order permeated with wisdom and harmony.

My journey to find the beautiful images I sought for my words took me, as it had for my previous book, *Healing Light*, to the incomparable Freer and Sackler Galleries. There I found an exquisite Hon'ami Koetsu scroll and screens, as well as stunning Kitagawa Sosetsu screens and rare eighteenth- to nineteenth-century Utaibon books, which allowed me to give life to my ideas through the unique beauty of Japanese art.

These meditations are an intensely personal representation of my observations of the gifts we have received and the paths we have taken. My prayer, as expressed in the opening poem, "Celestial Design," is that someday, in an enlightened era, humanity will choose to embrace earth's gift with a single heart.

Alexandra Villard de Borchgrave
Washington, D.C.

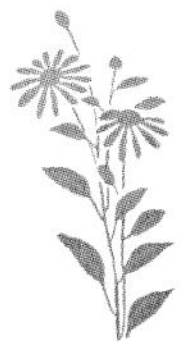

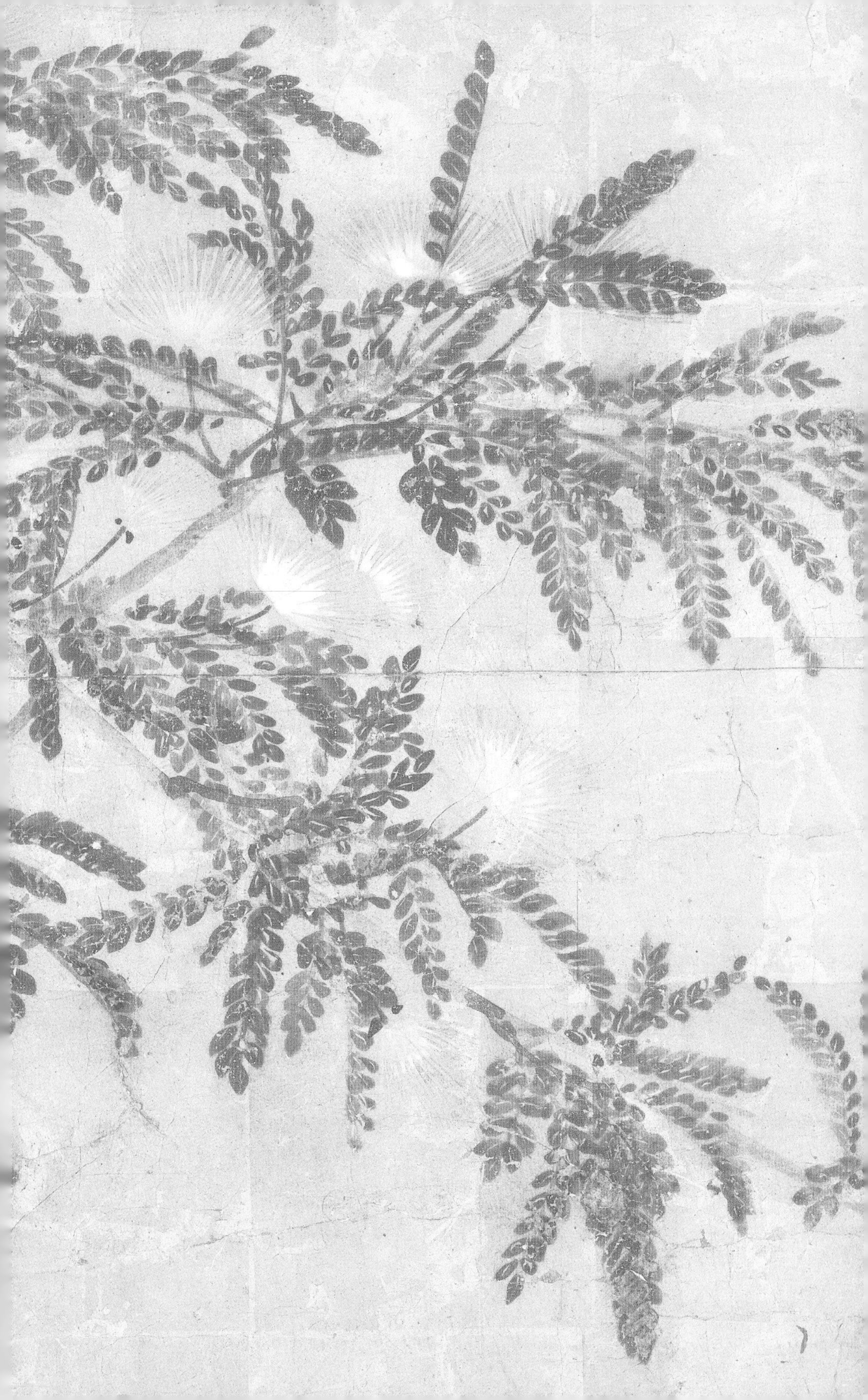

BEGINNING

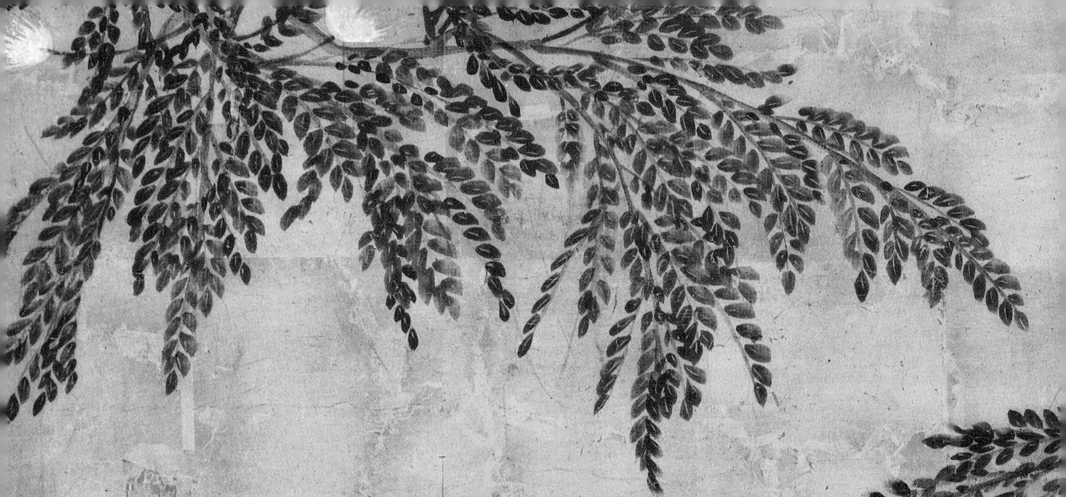

Celestial Design

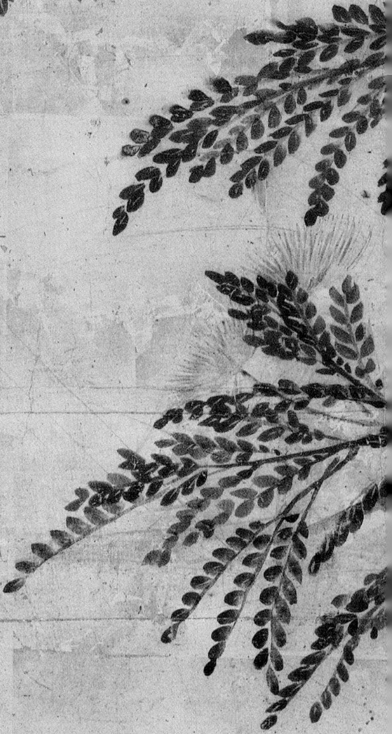

Beyond the stars
of the midnight hour,
A heavenly Spirit
of matchless power
Brushes the earth
with gold and blue
To infuse the world
with a luscious hue.

With dazzling strokes
of celestial design,
The mighty being
sets a stage divine
For beauty unparalleled
in a verdant grove
To reside in splendor
as a sacred trove.

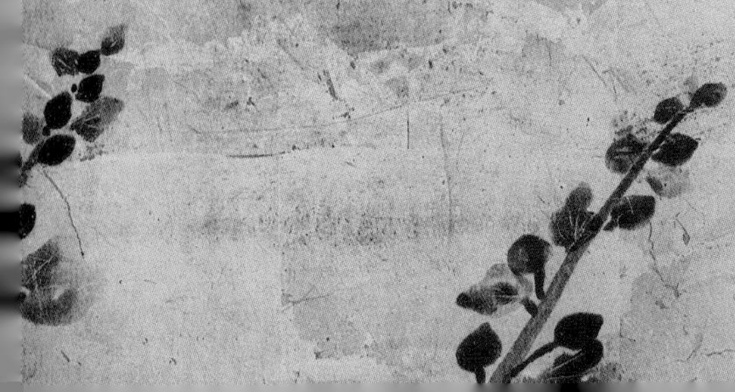

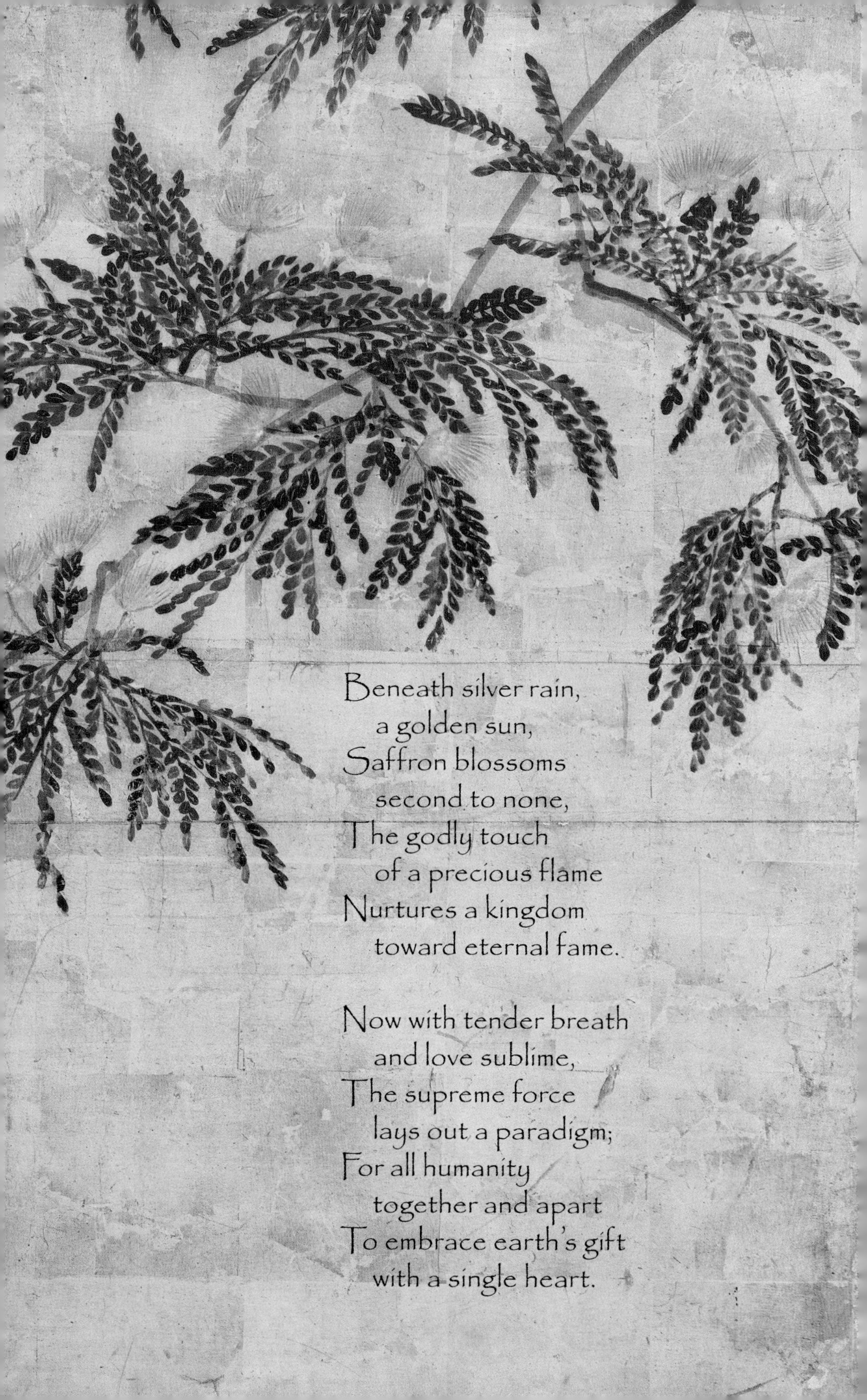

Beneath silver rain,
a golden sun,
Saffron blossoms
second to none,
The godly touch
of a precious flame
Nurtures a kingdom
toward eternal fame.

Now with tender breath
and love sublime,
The supreme force
lays out a paradigm;
For all humanity
together and apart
To embrace earth's gift
with a single heart.

HEAVENLY ORDER

Like a leaf floating
    upward in the wind,
The soul begins
    its search,
To find through
    heavenly order
The beauty of
    this earth.

The spirit pursues its
    passionate goal
With each flow of
    life's breath,
To reach the
    absolute beauty
That conquers
    even death.

The mind that beholds
    all beauties of time
Within its
    inner eye,
Achieves an
    immortality
Heaven would
    not deny.

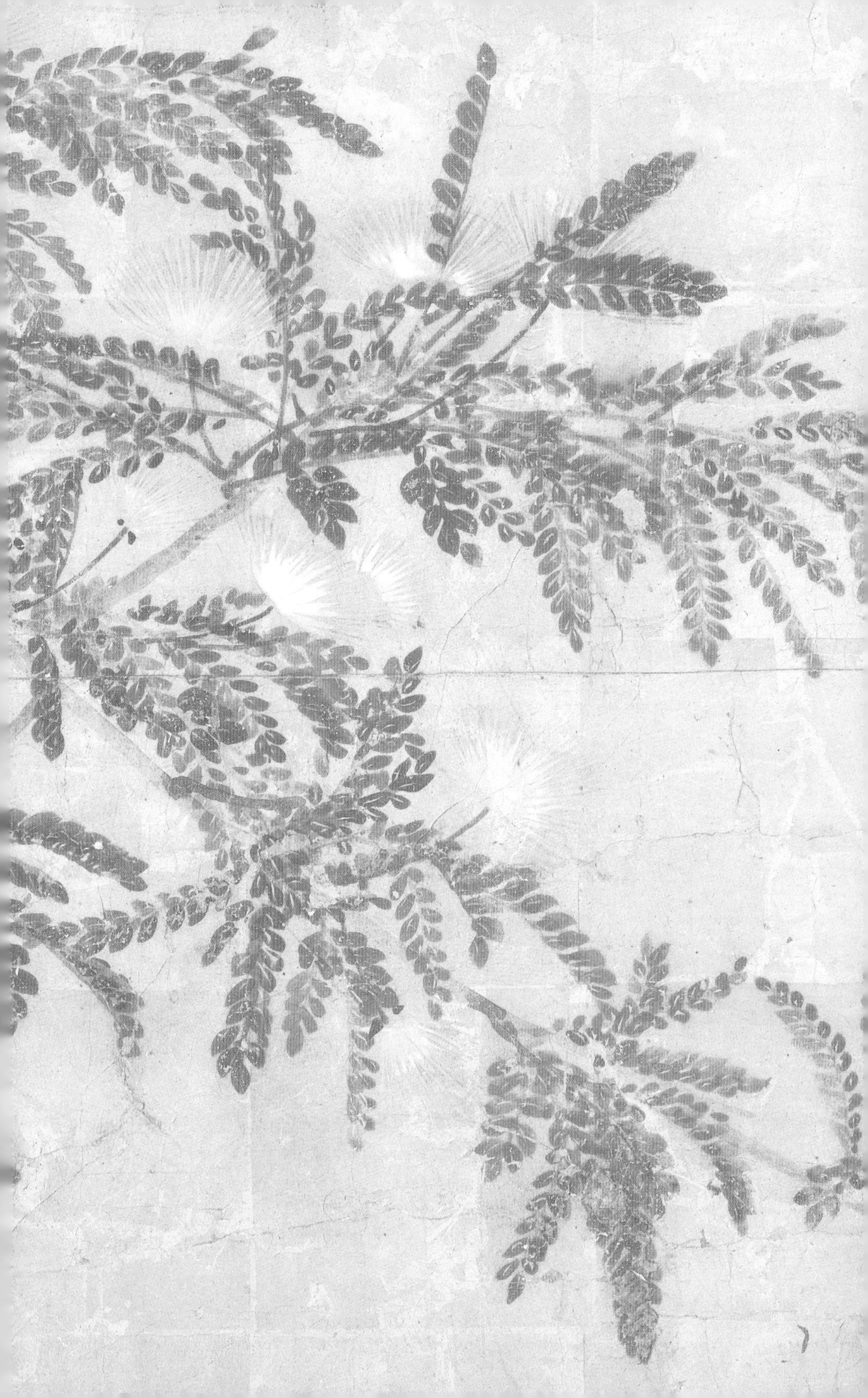

DARKNESS

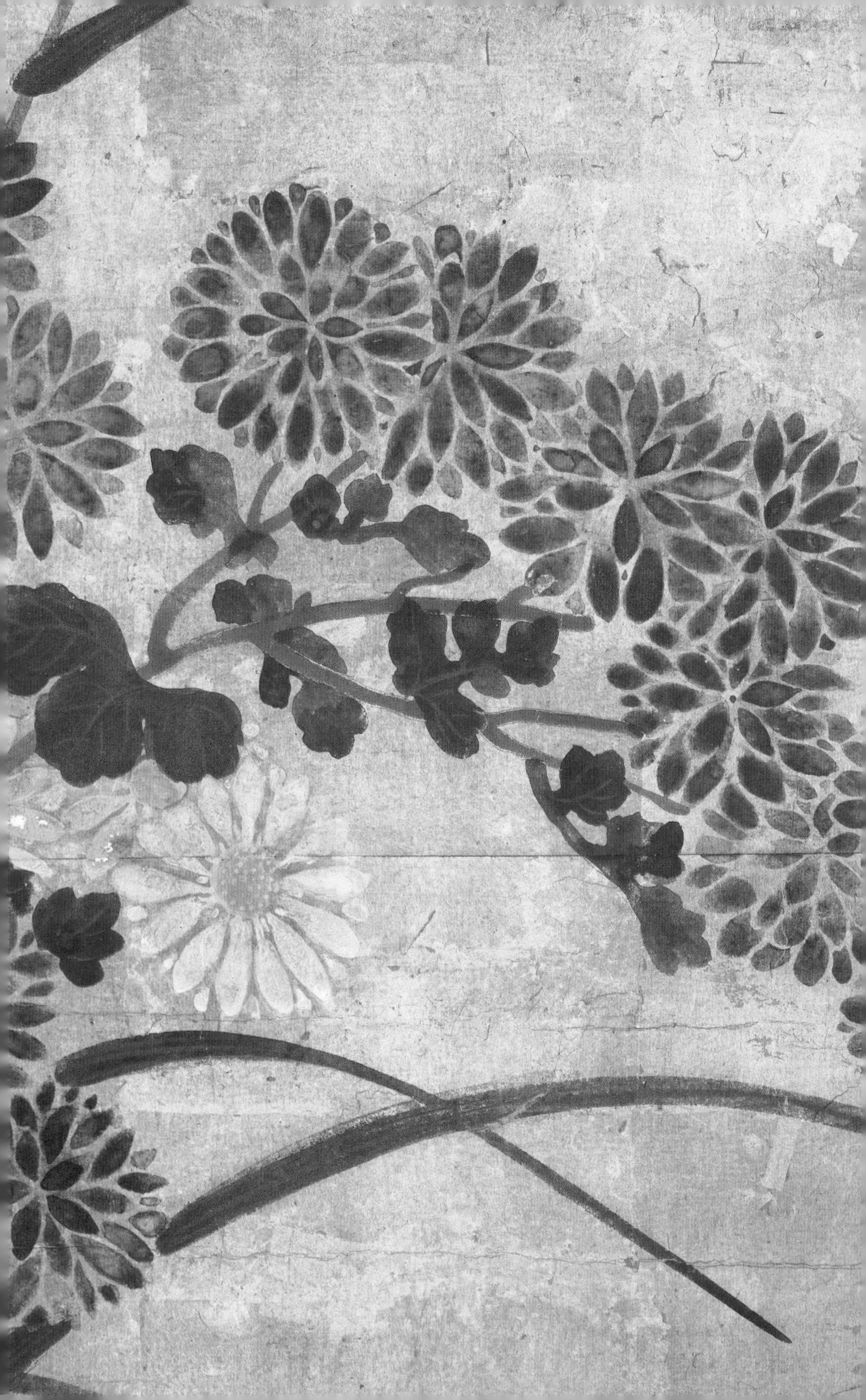

WAR

War is born
   of words ill spoken,
The descent to destruction paved
   with dreams now broken;
Noble intent paired
   with reckless guile
Leaves wisdom abandoned
   under scornful bile.
Shards of hope strewn
   on a treacherous path
Are crushed and lost
   amid mounting wrath.
As flames of anguish
   crackle and swell,
Forcing innocents and sinners
   into earthly hell,
Fresh tears of blood
   with dismay conspire
To challenge the will
   to defeat deeds most dire.
Yet deep within the remains
   of Samara's past glory,
Lie valuable lessons
   from an exalted story.

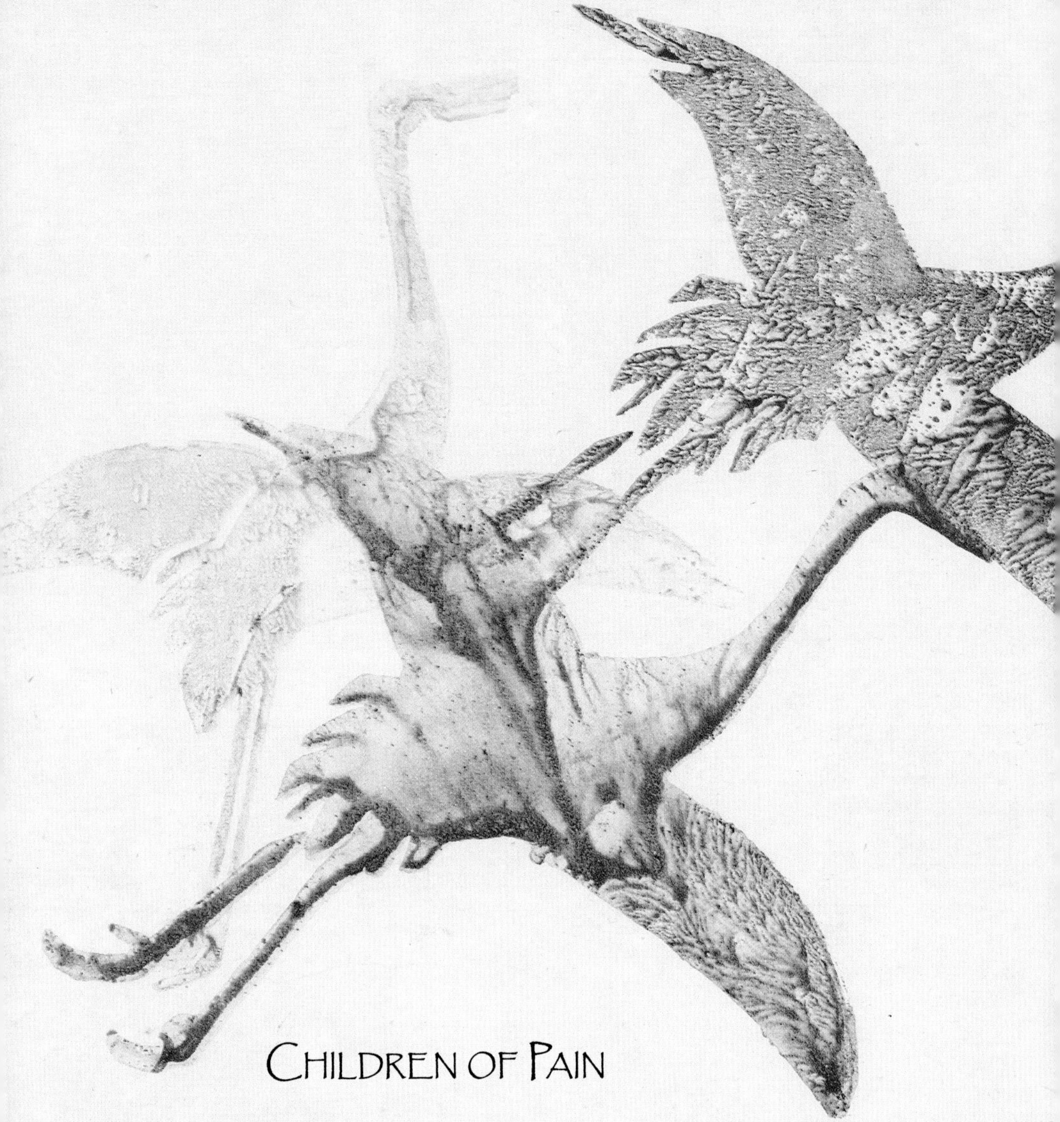

Children of Pain

Where goes this
icy dagger
But deep within
my heart,
To cut and tear with
cruel intent
And break my
soul apart?

Where can I find
    a refuge
From relentless
    searing pain,
When all about are
    shreds of truth
I struggle with
    in vain?

Where are the drops
    of wisdom
To cool my
    burning tears?
Perhaps I will only
    find them
Through a search of
    many years.

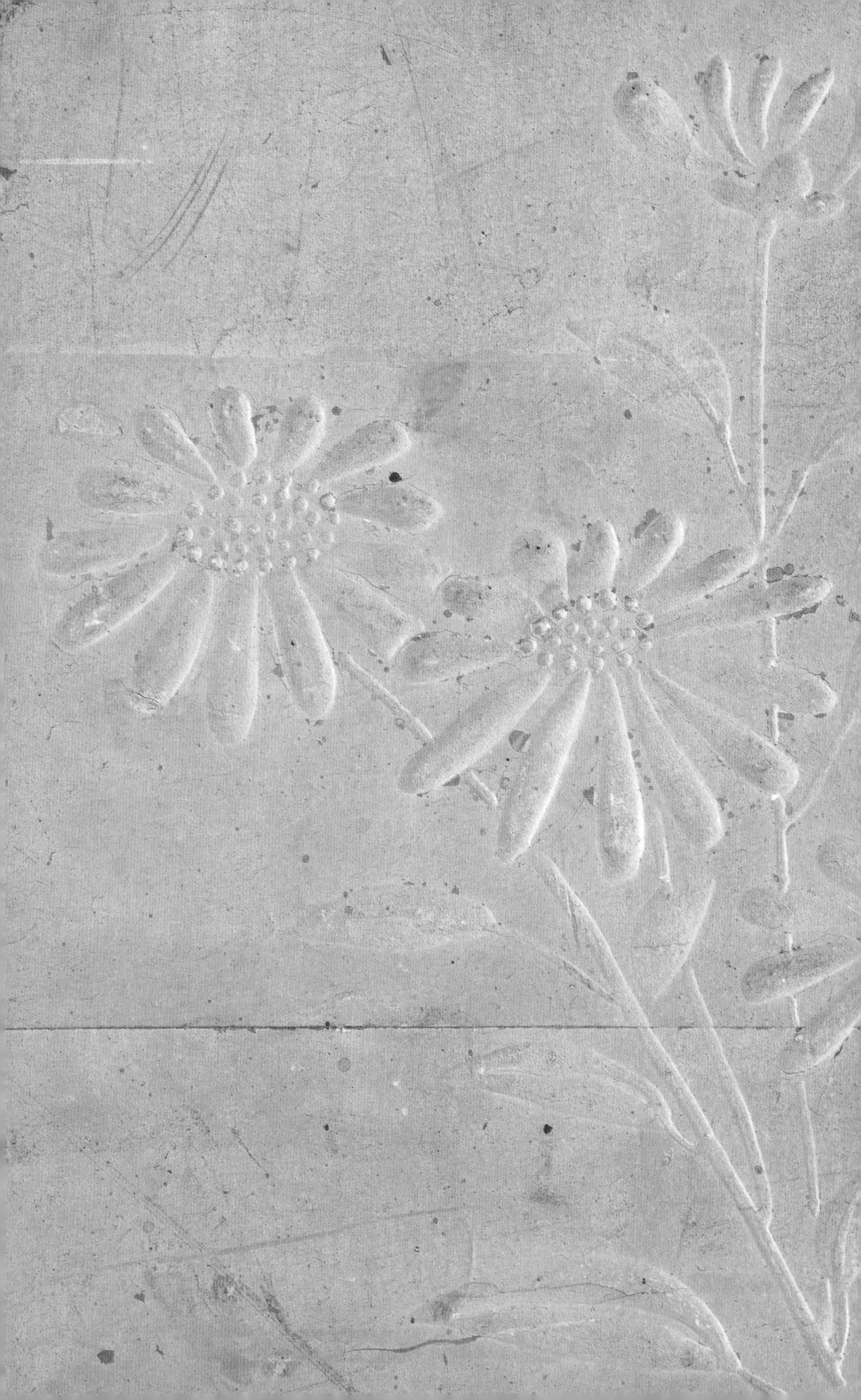

KINDNESS OF HEART

With all the world
   in disarray,
One tender blossom
   survives;
In the deepest crevasse
   of the human soul
The kindness of heart
   still thrives.

On a fragile stalk
   in a land of greed
A lone petal may turn
   in the cold,
To touch one life
   with a gift of warmth
Bringing hope
   more needed than gold.

A blazing instant
   in a moonless night
Transforms misery and woe
   into fire;
Where darkness prevailed
   in a wretched sty,
Now tenderness allows life
   to transpire.

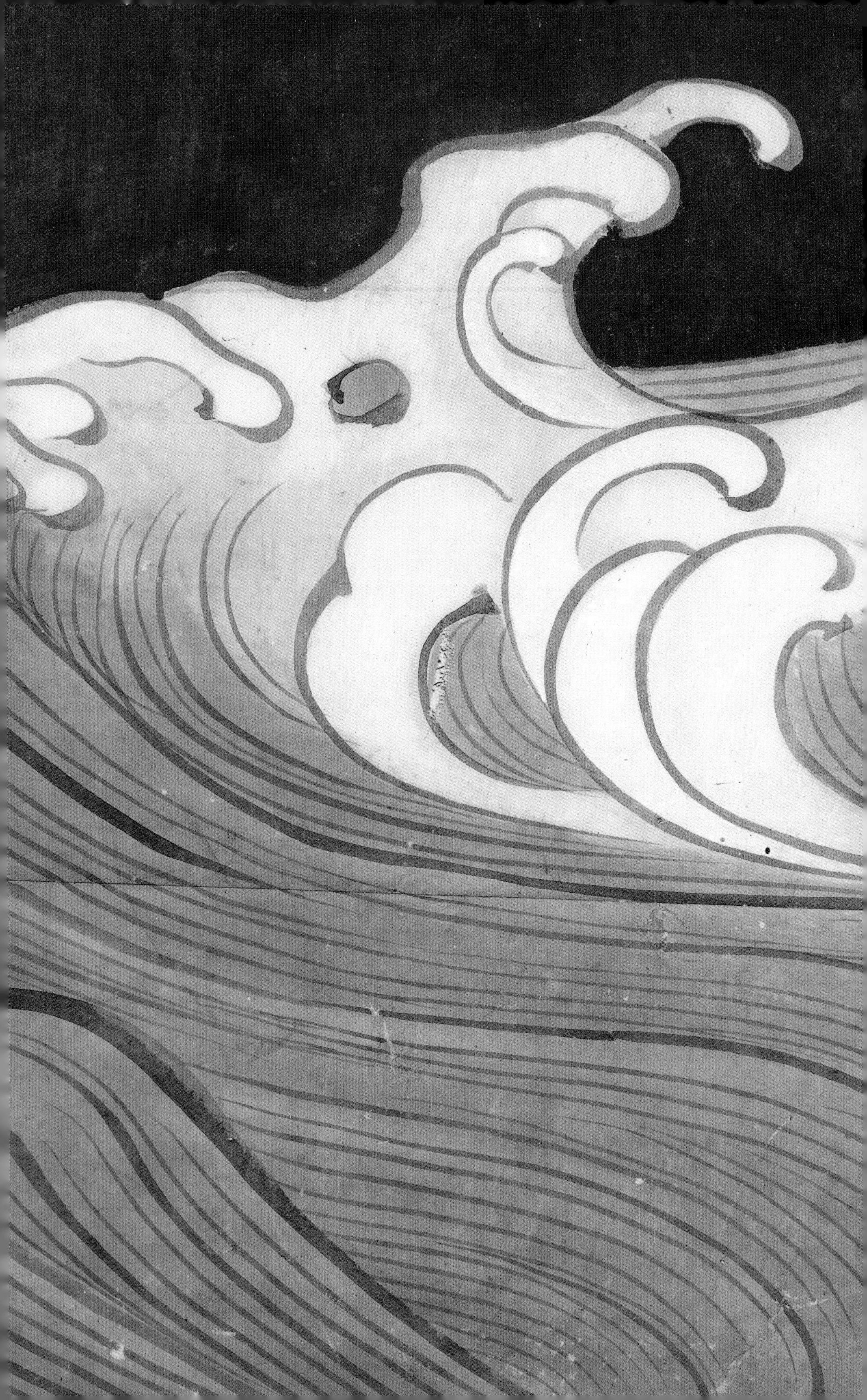

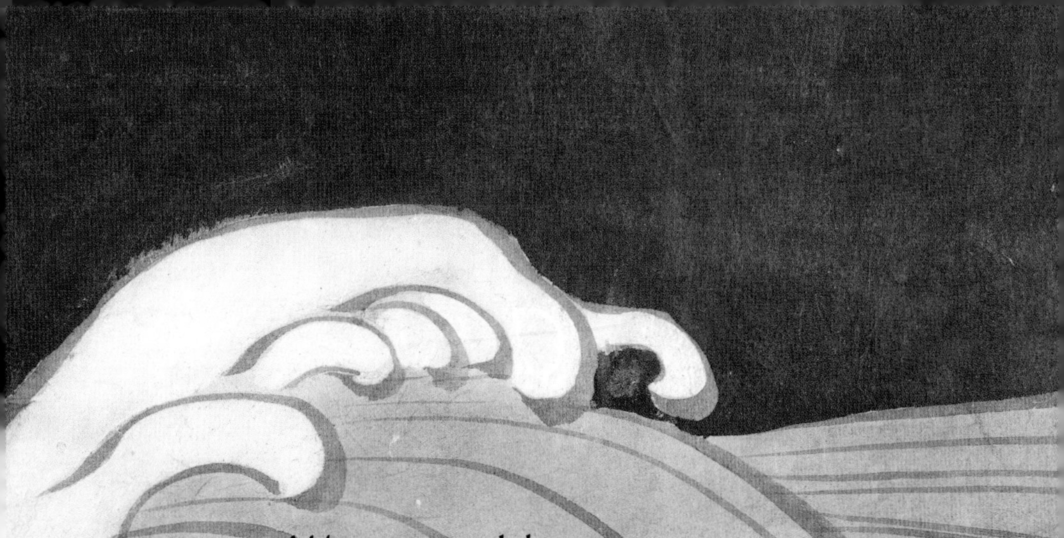

WAVES OF HUNGER

A thousand desires may consume the mind
  in a ceaseless, yearning quest;
Sending waves of hunger
  against sands of time
Without hope
  for the soul to rest.

With each new whim a wave is born
  to quench the arid land
Where thirst for bliss
  may never be slaked
And illusion
  makes a perilous stand.

What purpose can the soul now find
  in the current of discontent?
To seek release
  in the flow of life
Through the wonder
  of the world's firmament.

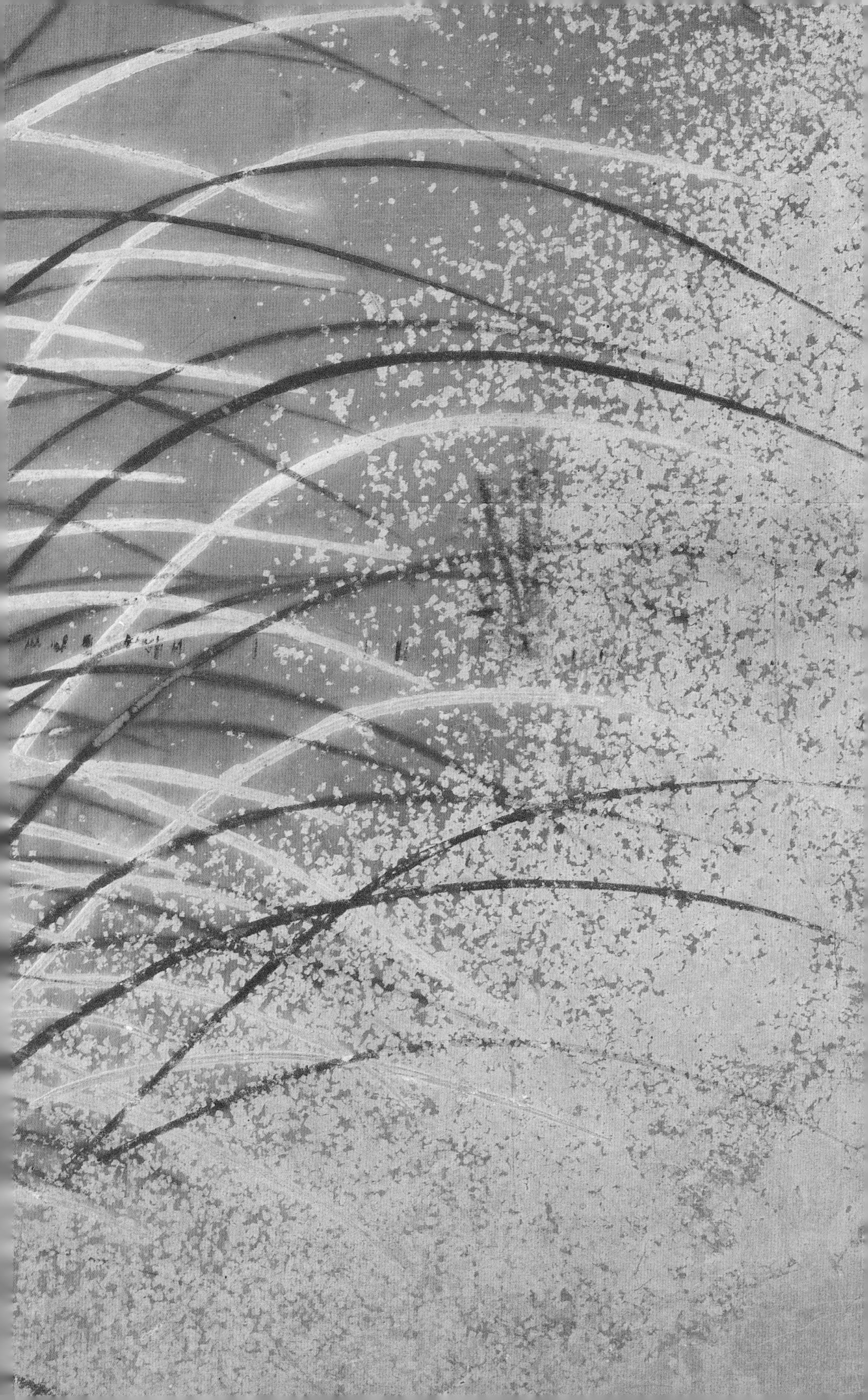

LEAVES OF HOPE

The story starts
    with leaves of hope
That sprout from
    the heart of the earth,
Singing a verse
    to all the world
Of love and faith
    and man's true worth.

While mud may spatter
    the single leaf,
The sun not touch it
    for a day,
Its dreams of life
    defy the storm
To reach clear heights,
    come what may.

Though buds may grow
    with touching feats
To wilt in the moon's
    cold eclipse,
The will to rise
    with fresh resolve
Is the song on each
    petal's lips.

Chains of Fear

The dark of night bears
swiftly down
To fill the heart
with dread;
For in this bleakest
hour of time
Lies the path the soul
fears to tread.

Like scavenging crows
the swords of grief
Reveal memories of
a thousand lives;
Where errors committed
from rage and gall
Defeat goodness while
evil survives.

Throughout struggle and strife
the chains of fear
Trap the soul in a
well of despair;
But inside the heart dwells
the strength of a god
To pull wisdom from
the cry of a prayer.

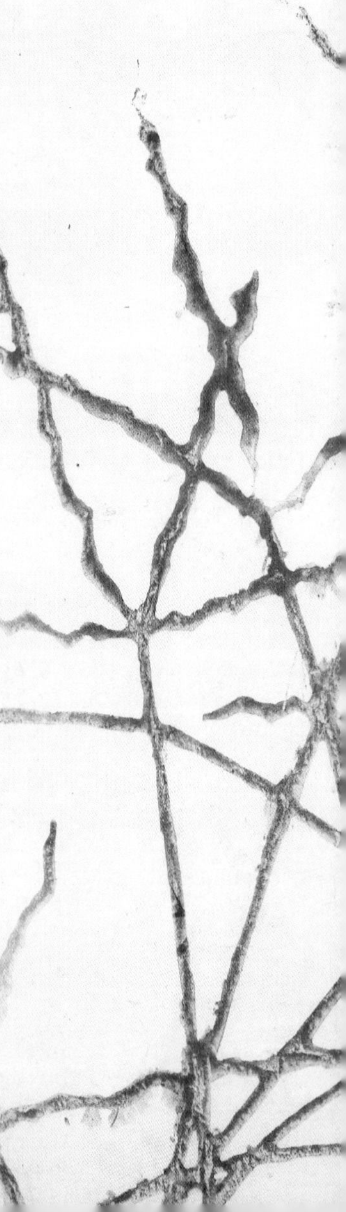

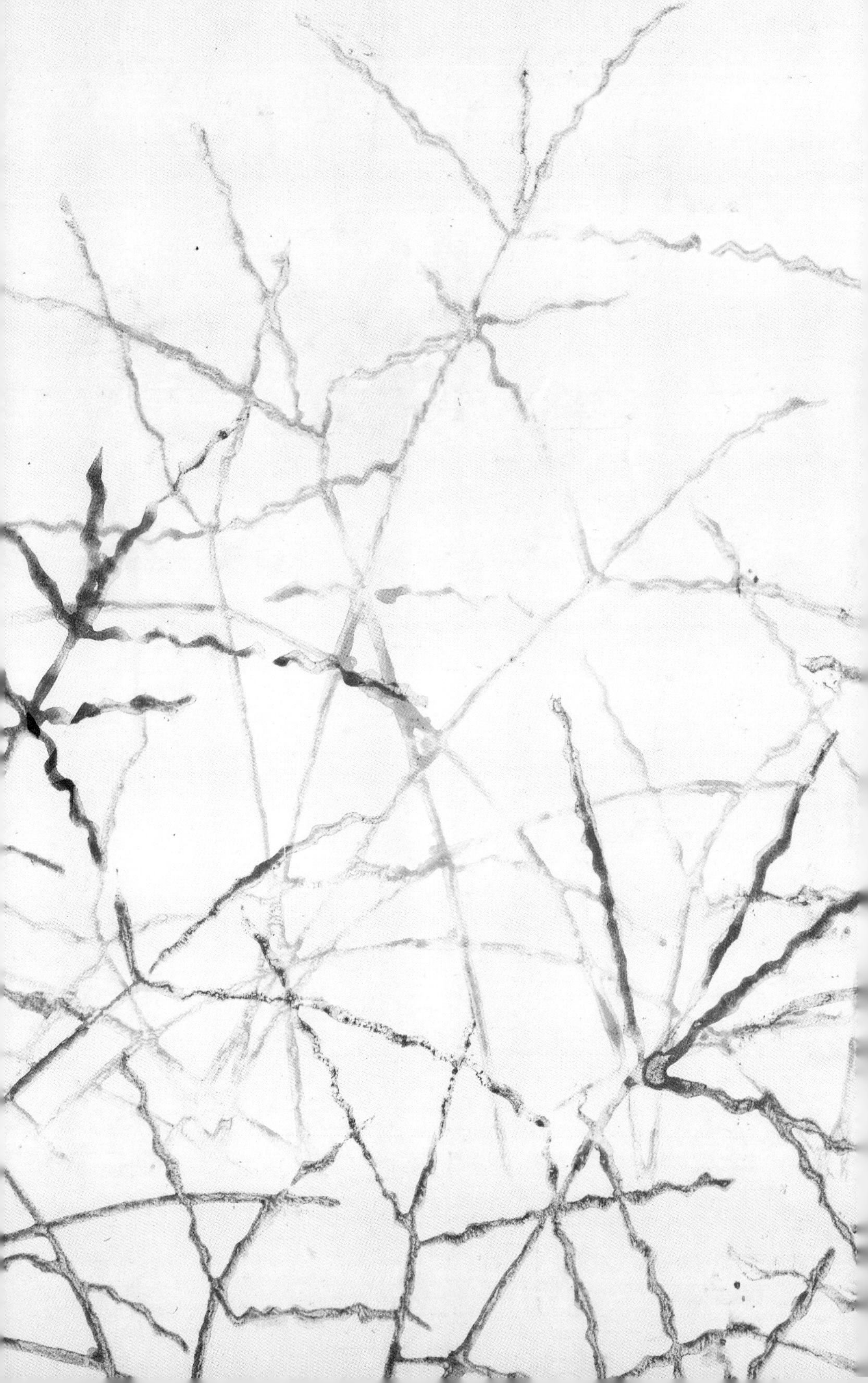

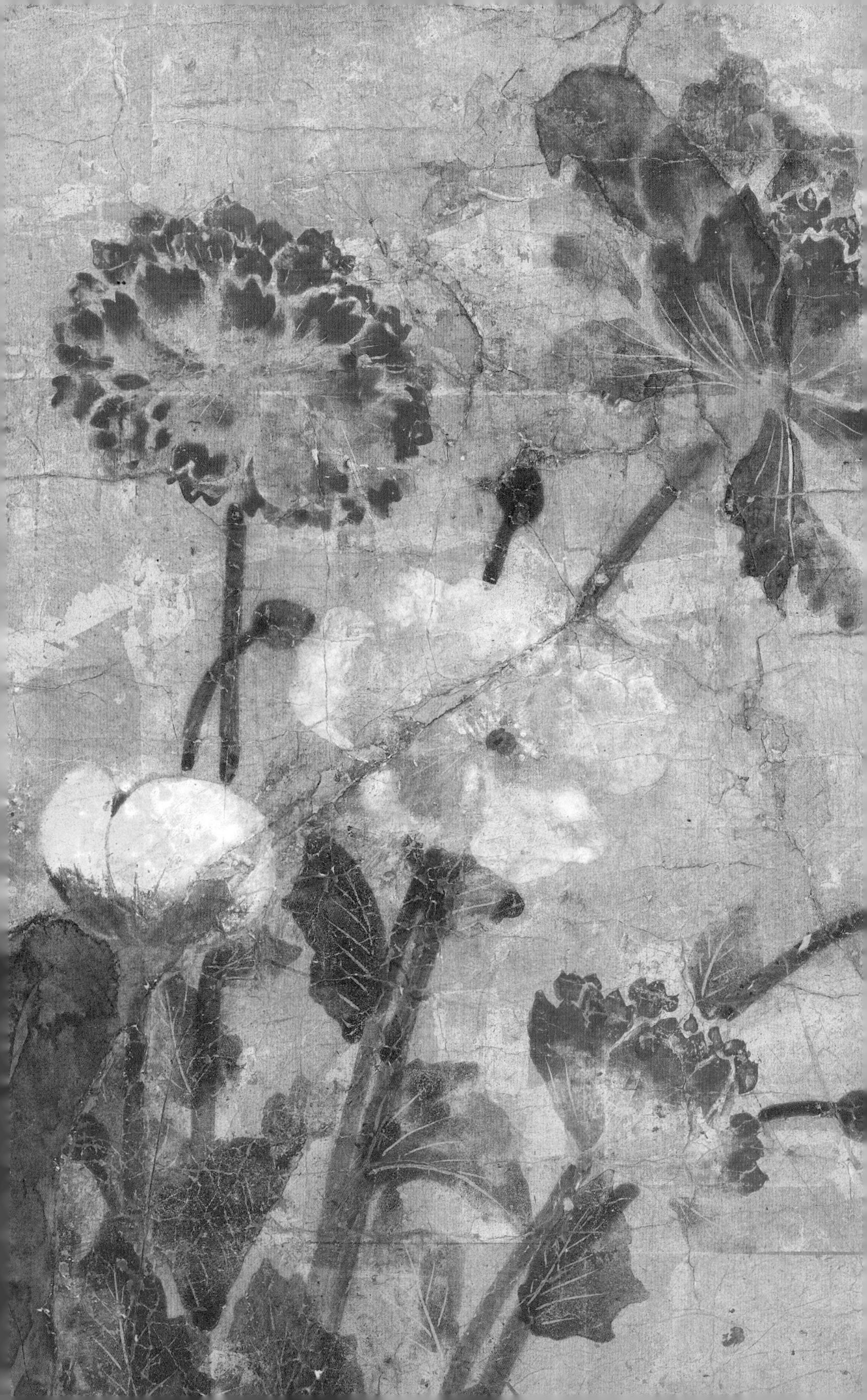

SPIRIT OF VALOR

The spirit that lies
  in every heart
Ascends
  with a radiant light,
And the human will
  to love and aspire
Brings the promise
  to achieve and excite.

Like a shooting star
  in a fading sky,
Courage
  within can prevail,
Leading us
  from a path of hate
To a peace,
  however frail.

While the breaking dawn
  may not reveal
The heavenly sight
  we seek;
It may, in its glory,
  herald the rise of
True valor in
  all its mystique.

CLOUDS OF ANGER

Clouds of anger
    dim the clarity of sight
When a storm of arrogance
    stirs an unholy fight.
As wings of conceit beat against
    the pulse of life,
Time runs out for those
    caught in the strife.
Misplaced energy leaves
    blood in the dust,
To be swept by a wind
    that betrays all trust.
While the drive to impose
    a universal claim
Plunges downward like lightening
    heedless of whom it may maim,
Lone saplings of reason
    are lost to a wrong
And must bend in the gale,
    revealing roots that are strong.

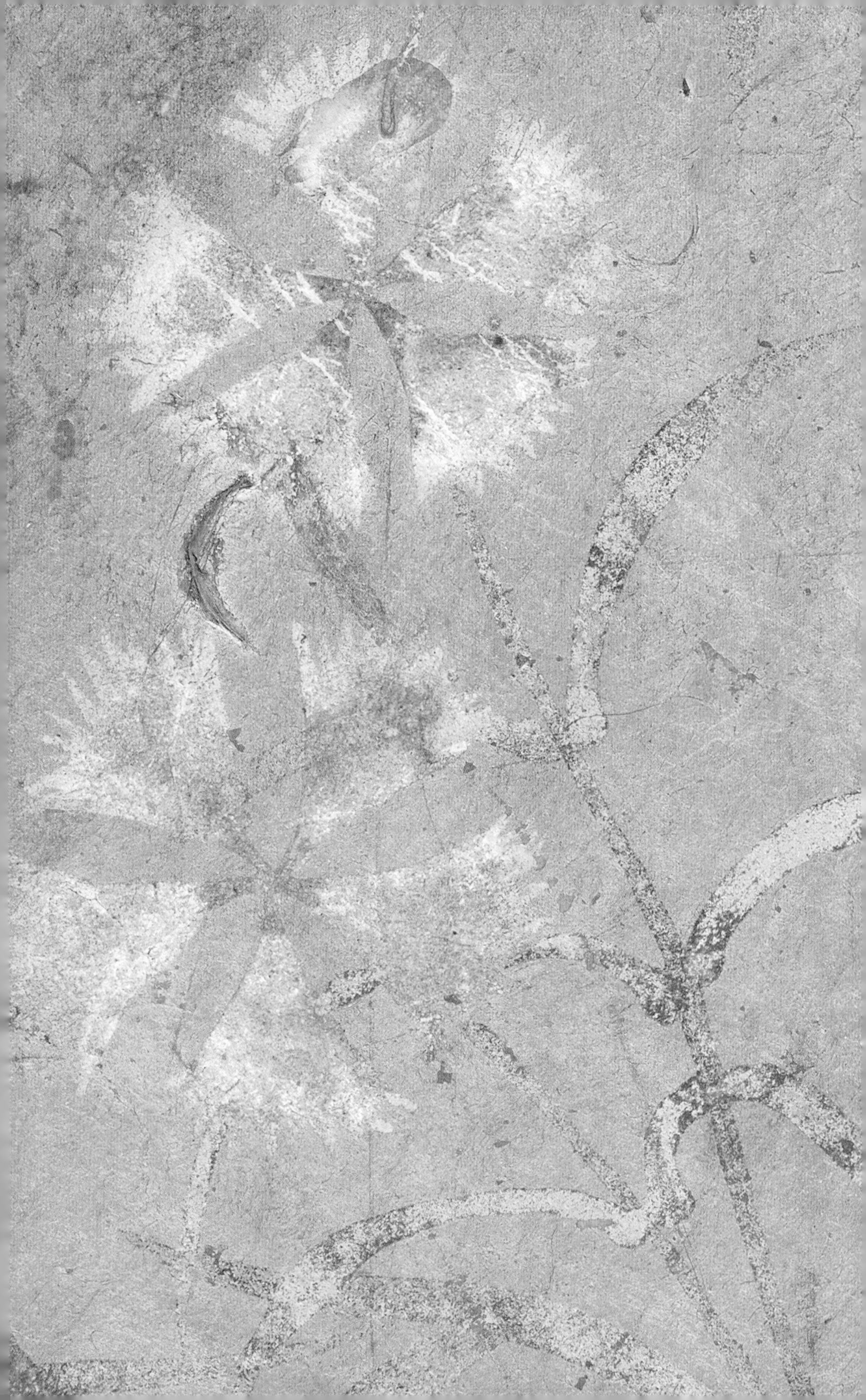

PASSION FOR FAIRNESS

How can we find
   a passion
For fairness in
   this life,
And choose a
   path of beauty
Over cruelty
   and strife?

How can we search
   the ruins
Of majesty
   and grace,
And find new ways
   of legend
To overcome
   disgrace?

How can we reach
   that realm,
Beyond all
   shattered dreams,
Where peace
   becomes the water
Of cooling,
   healing streams?

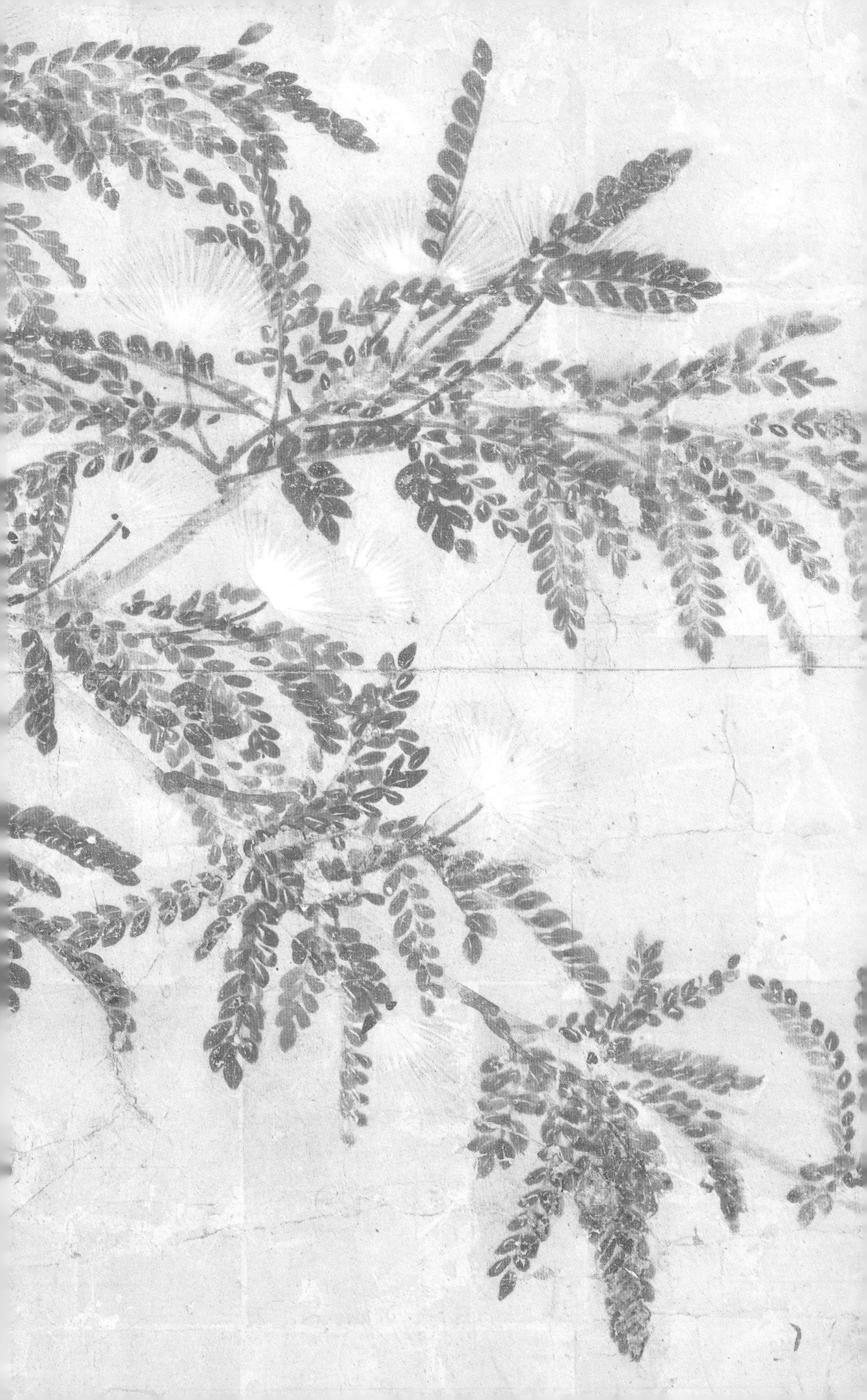

HUMANITY

SHELTER

Like the weariness of night
    passivity sets in
While inhumanity to man
    engulfs the world in sin;
The shadows of pain
    stretch far without blame
And blows are dealt freely with
    no sense of shame.
One soul may take flight
    to find shelter from death,
Delivered by the mercy of
    a single caring breath.
Another might fall in
    a crueler fashion,
Among rocks of despair and
    unrealized passion.
From the earth soaked with tears
    a new spirit must arise,
To petition our conscience for
    a call to be wise.

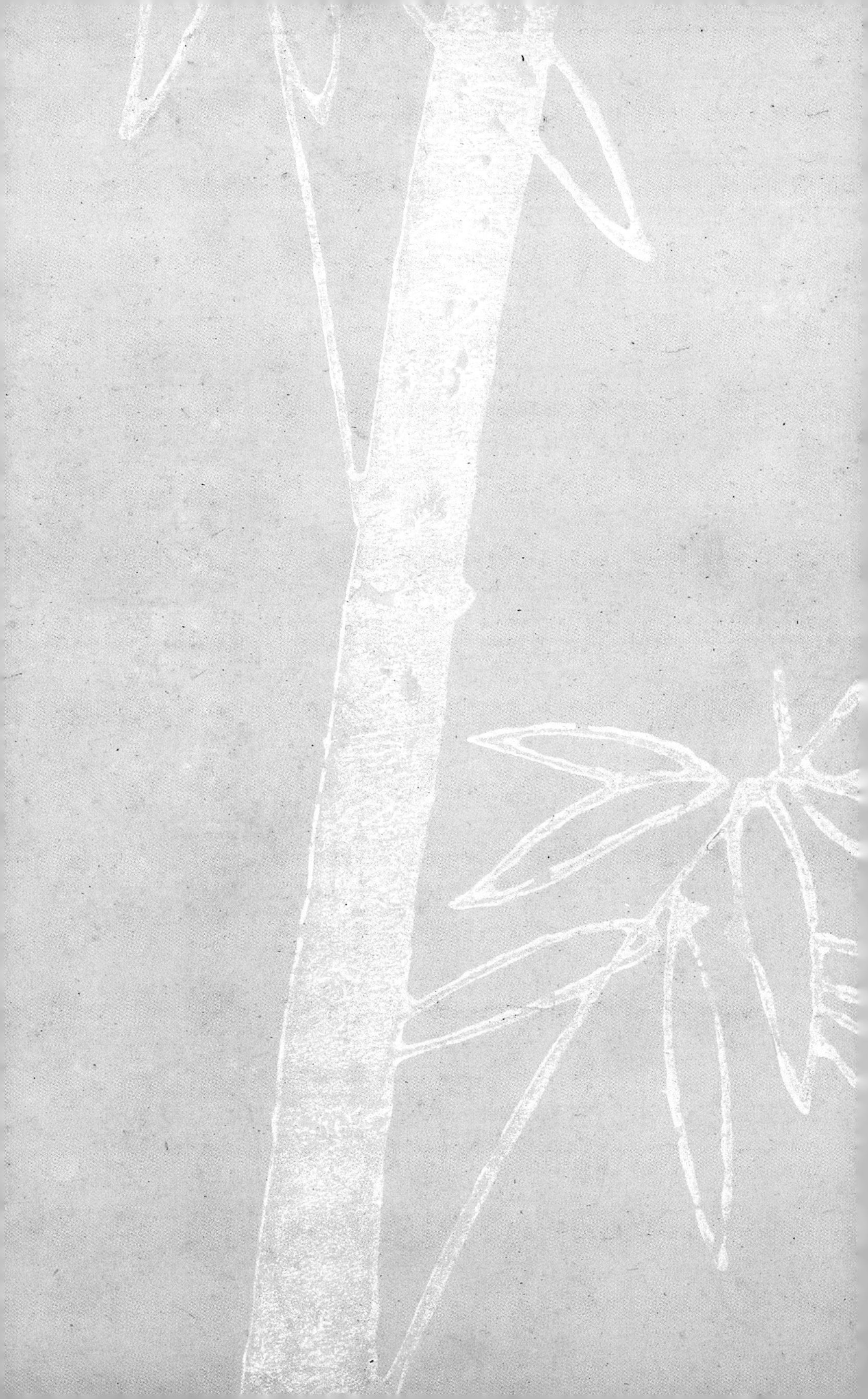

A Sea of Tranquility

A sea of tranquility
  lies deep and still
In the core
  of the human soul;
Where the soundless depth
  of the treasure of life
Is found in
  small fragments made whole.

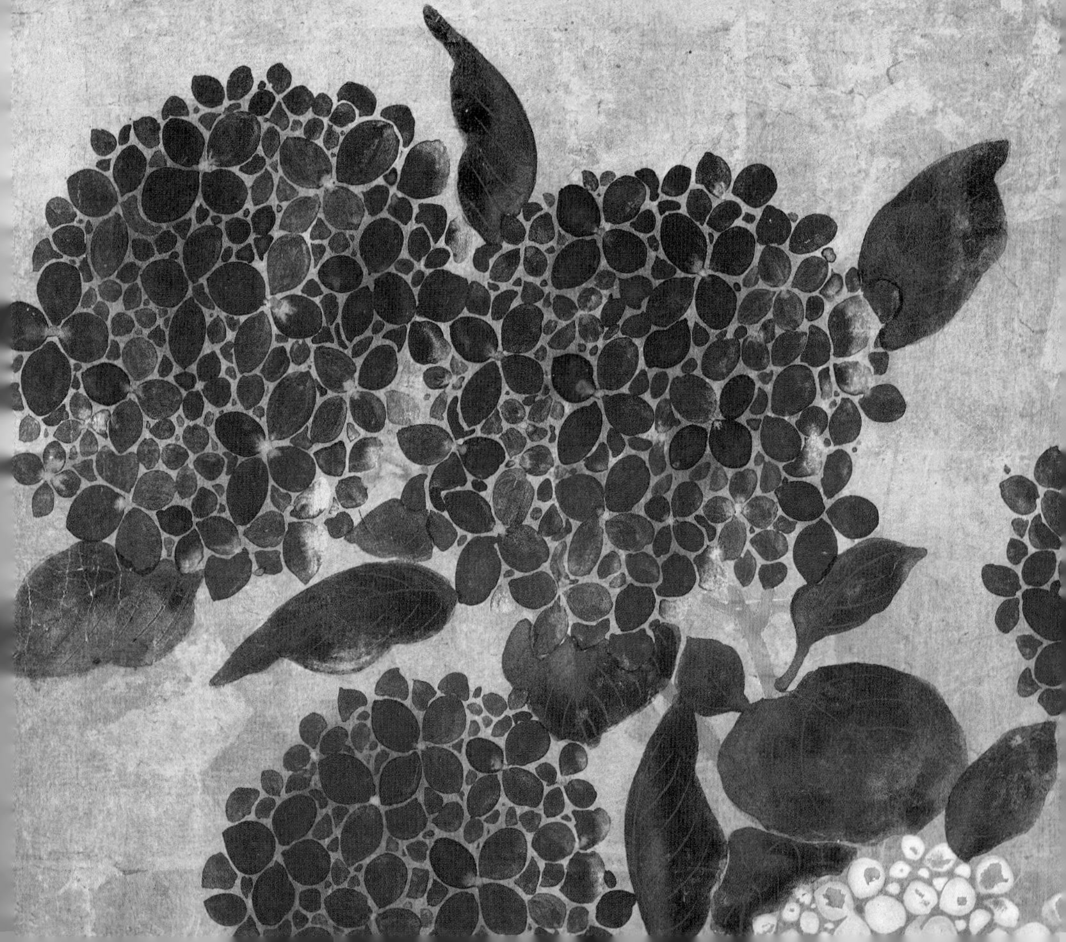

The search for harmony
through a tide of faith
Leads the heart over
waves of flaws;
To see humility in
a grain of sand
Resides at
the crux of the cause.

The purity of love carries
crests of light
To create peace for
all mankind;
For in the hidden shoals
of wisdom and strength
Dwell the keys to
hearts that are kind.

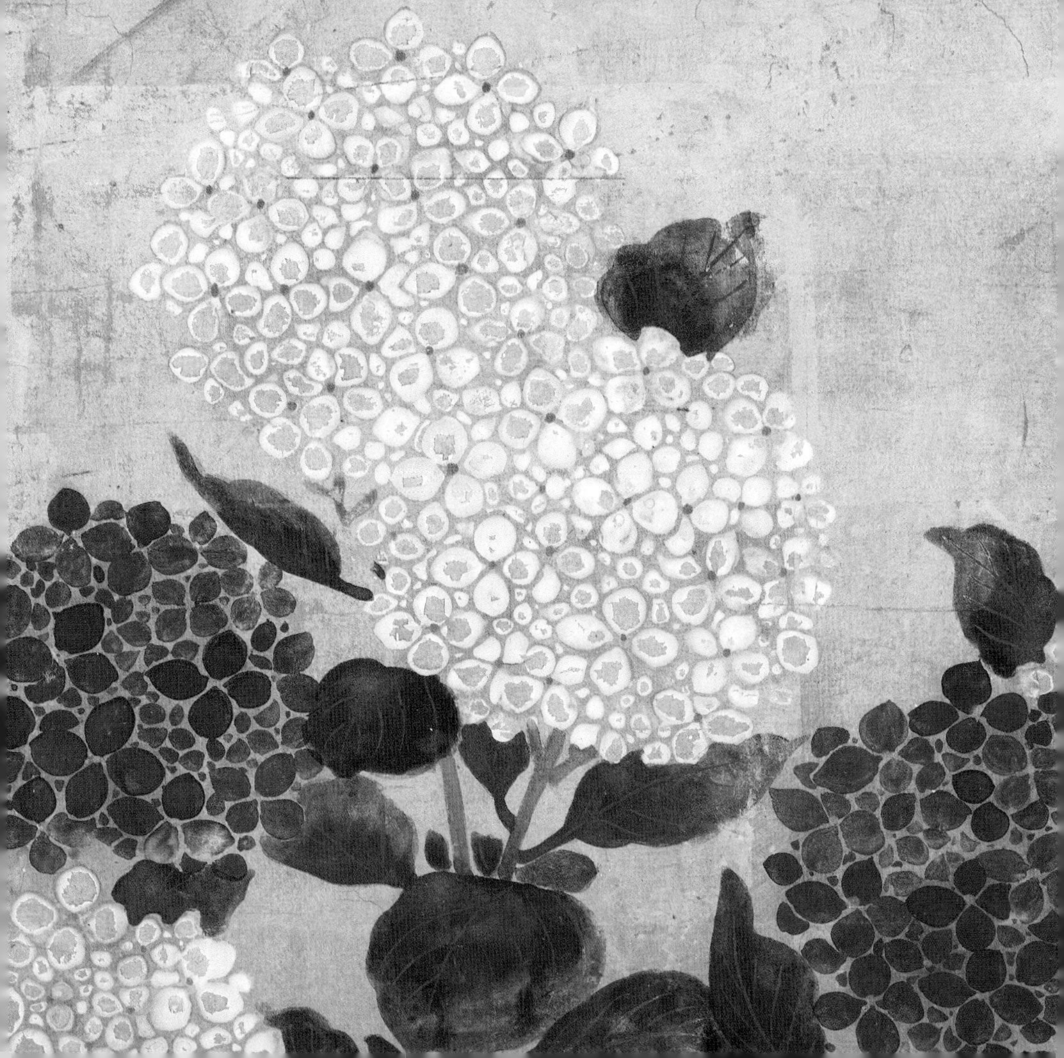

PURSUIT OF RAPTURE

Blissful skies
   entreat the heart
To play with visions
   in the wind,
Yet a burst of joy,
   like a ray of sun,
Disappears as the
   day must rescind.

The thrilling chase of a
   butterfly in flight
Draws us upward through
   branches of dreams,
To alight at the top of
   a tree of hope
To capture the
   moon's silver beams.

The pursuit of rapture
   with each worldly act
Opens new paths of
   golden respite,
Too soon overtaken by
   shadows of truth
Leading the soul down
   the course into night.

PETALS OF JOY

Petals of joy open
     into the sun
To reach for life's
     glorious light,
Transporting the heart
     on a journey of love
For a flower's sweet
     scent of delight.

The beauty in this
     spirit for life
Is unique to the
     human soul;
Its infinite capacity
     to rise into flight
Takes it far beyond
     a single goal.

While thistles and thorns
     may thwart each turn,
Elation speeds the heart
     on its way
To find new radiance
     in a blaze of perfection
No pain can
     ever allay.

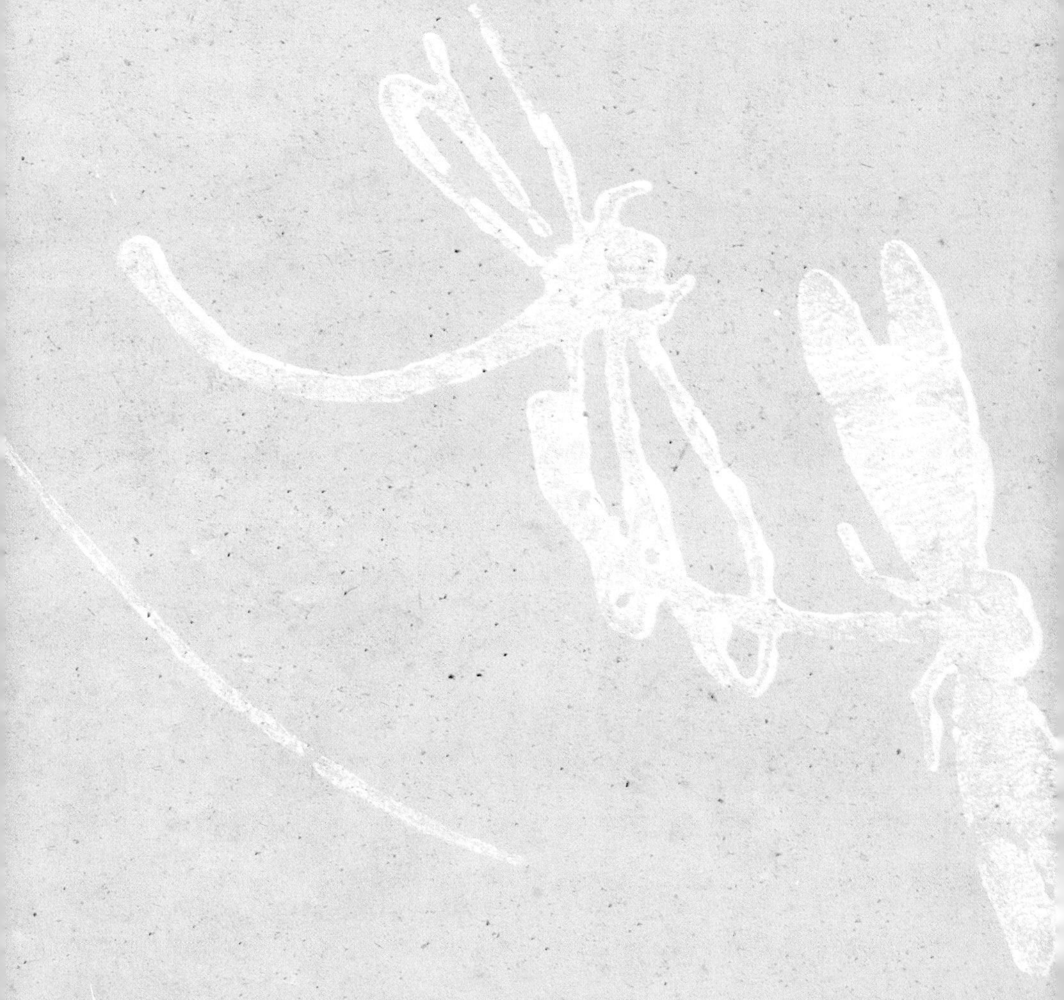

TORN HEART

A torn heart casts out
   thoughts of love
And wanders among
   willows of distress;
Desire, regret, both
   passion and restraint
Churn the senses with
   the need to regress.

Memories intrude –
   past lost dreams –
In intriguing encounters
   that invite,
Giving hope to a soul
   battered by fears
To revive in the heavens'
   soft light.

The mystery of love
   weaves in and out
In a magical,
   complex skein,
Twisting strands of despair
   with those of joy
Until the heart finds
   a peace unforeseen.

FORGIVENESS

Call forth the stars from
   a pale twilight sky
To will the heart to
   ask for calm inside,
For in the passing of
   day into night,
Lies the hope for
   forgiveness to preside.

Surrender to the mercy
    of deep peace
To be found in the
    vastness of earth's time,
Where hatred and woe
    may be dissolved
Into the notes of love's
    infinite chime.

BEYOND EARTH'S RIM

Each step across a blade of grass
    brings learning in its wake,
With fresh desire for greater strength
    to win a higher stake.

The path must flow with bold attempts
    to stretch beyond earth's rim,
And reach the edge of heaven's gate
    with patience for a hymn.

Resilience now may lead the soul
    to grow with inner grace,
Drawing genius from its depth
    to burst with ardent pace.

The vines that hang with wondrous blooms
    reflect that perfect state,
Where beauty in its rarest form
    is free to meet its fate.

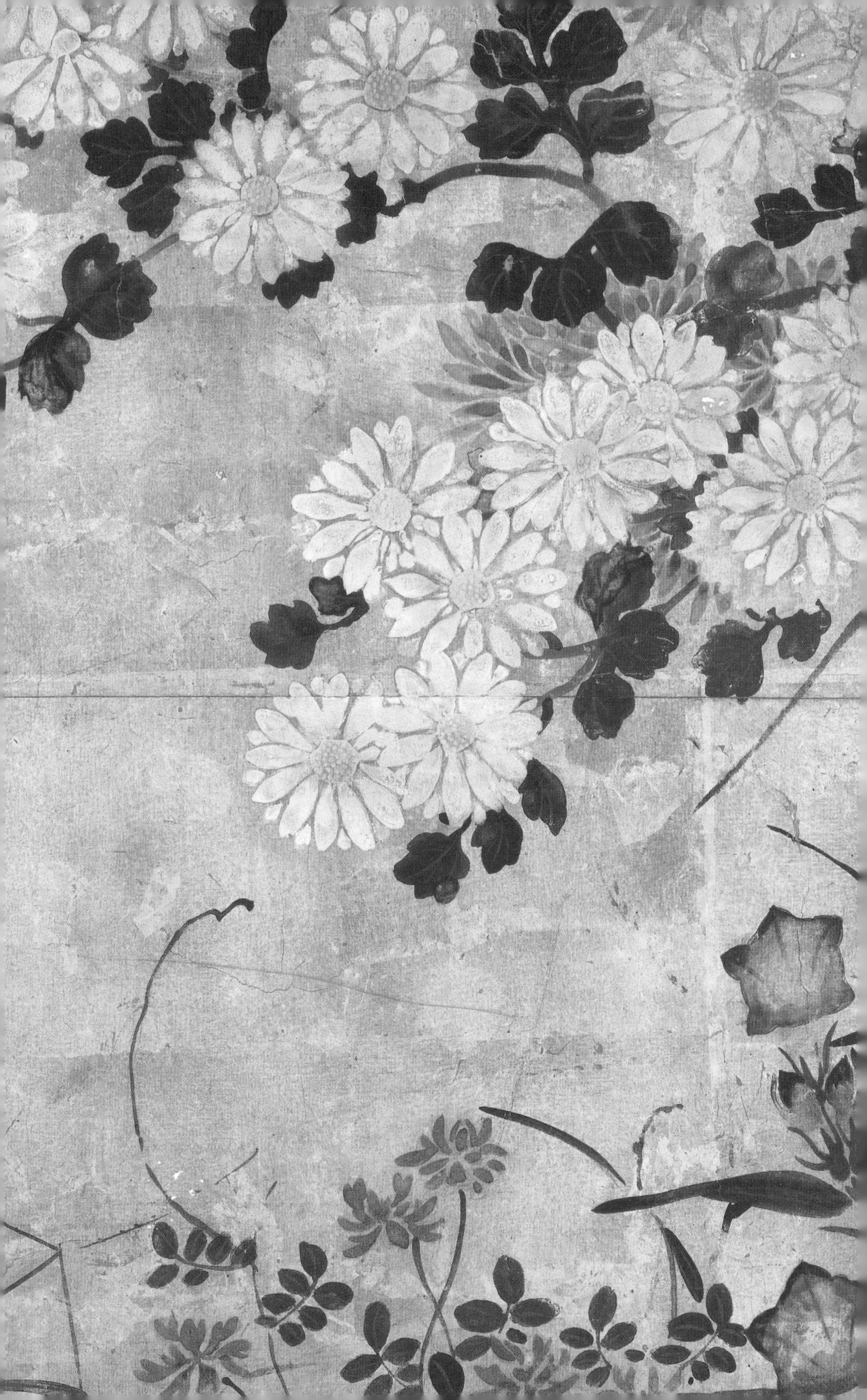

MIST OF LOVE

The finest clouds
   of light stand still
To greet love's birth
   at dawn;
For from this lustrous
   source of life,
Pure greatness may
   be drawn.

The mist of love
   climbs in the heat
Of passion
   at its height,
With silver threads
   of hope to guide
The dream
   in soaring flight.

Midst pain and joy,
   the heart's grand quest
Moves the soul
   beyond its fate;
To find in lovers'
   immortal realm,
The secret of
   love's true state.

SEARCHING

Whatever the road
   one takes in life,
Let it lead past
   the selfish mind;
While tears may fall
   like leaves on a pond,
May stems of great
   longing unwind.

Though each step may
   try the bravest heart,
True purpose now
   wakens the need
To reach the shore
   of enlightened sight
With the strength to build
   a new creed.

The secret world of
   the searching heart
Is opened by
   a loving glance,
Allowing hidden dreams
   of the soul
To spire into
   limitless chance.

KNOTS OF ARROGANCE

Knots of arrogance
　　halt the flow of life
When kindly endeavors
　　could end the strife;
Ill will corrodes
　　the spirit into rust,
Leaving contempt in place
　　of healing trust.

Ropes of devotion bind
　　those divided,
Resolving quarrels
　　still undecided;
For life must soon find
　　the eternal night
Filling the heart with
　　longing to requite.

Rays of Compassion

Let reason pour forth
over stones of doubt
To release the soul
from dismay,
Showing the clearest
path to the divine
Although clouds of pain
slow the way.

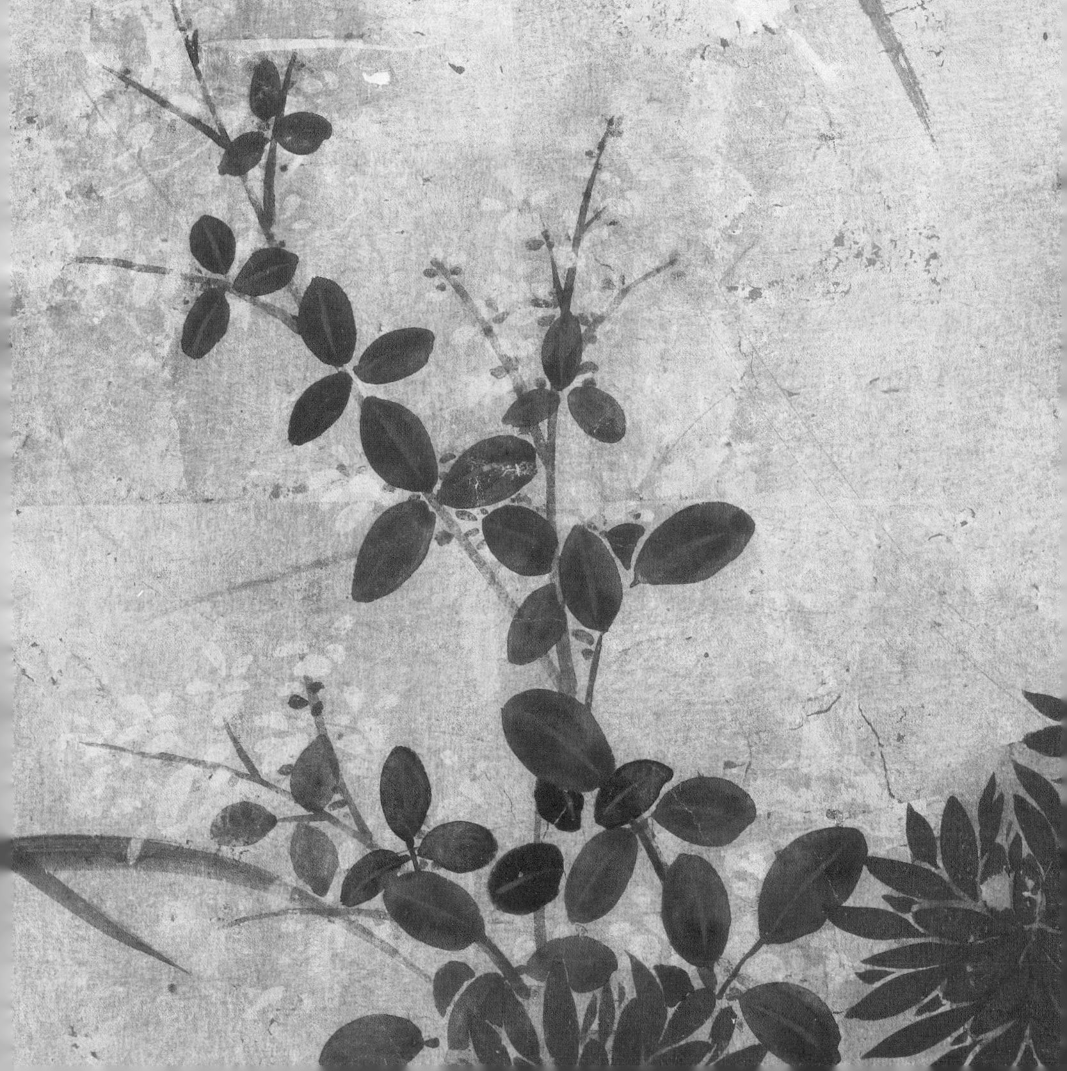

Sacrifice of self,
  mercy to others,
Give wings to the
  heart's deep desire:
Extend humanity
  with gracious might
Just as night turns
  to morning fire.

Luminous rays of
  compassion consume
The soul, now refined
  to a flame,
With burning thirst
  to help all in despair
Arise with compelling
  new aim.

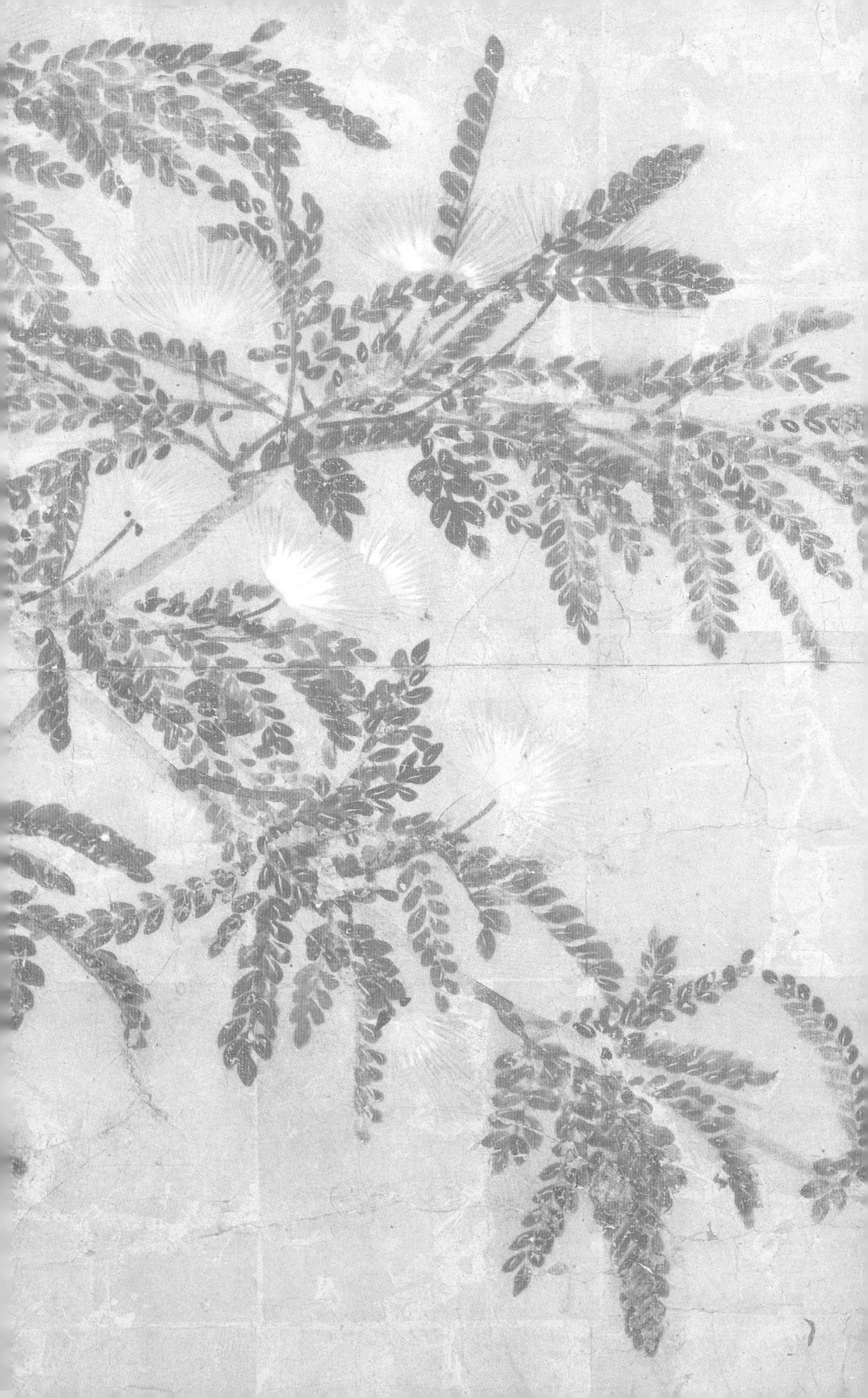

LIGHT

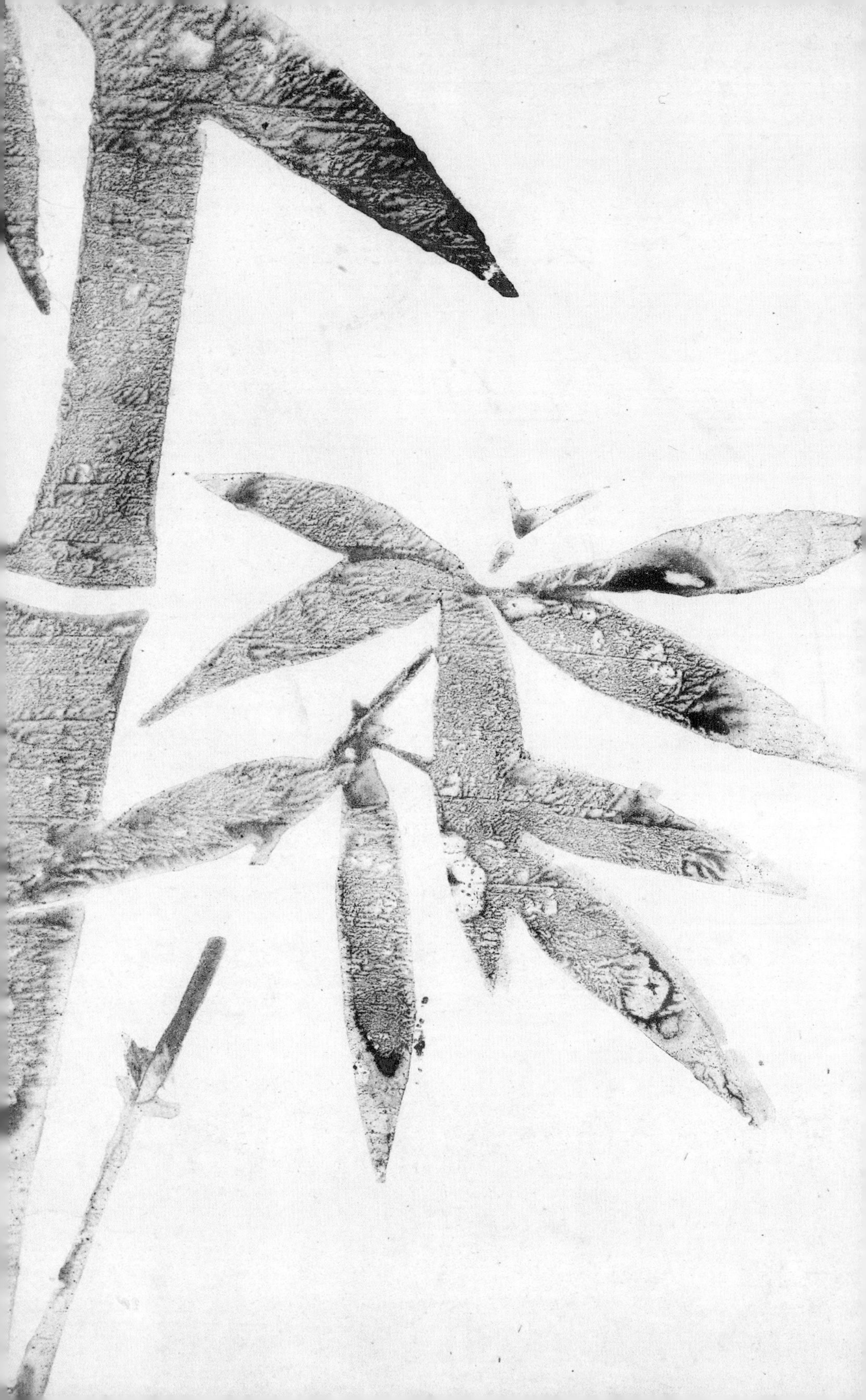

PATH TO WISDOM

As the fern unfolds into
    morning light,
The soul also seeks
    lucidness of sight;
From each valued sphere of
    sorrow and joy,
A thousand new flares of
    wisdom deploy.

The spirit journeys amid
    grief and pain,
Yet honest mistakes instill
    graceful gain;
The soul now searching for
    assuaging peace,
Finds courage within
    truth's heady release.

Redress lies in a love
    that surpasses
The sadness of life's
    grievous trespasses;
While windows to love may
    open and close,
Faith will forever
    shine through in repose.

BLOSSOM OF HOPE

Dark forces gather
   to challenge the world,
Banners of evil
   newly unfurled;
But a fragile blossom
   of hope may prevail
To hold in the wind,
   survive the hail.

On the highest cliff
   above the sea,
A beacon burns bright
   for eternity;
With courage unrivaled
   in the face of fear
To inspire the dreams
   of those who draw near.

The wisdom of life
   is stronger than dread
Of the forces that
   now seem widespread;
While mortals may tremble
   at squalls from above
They also possess
   the unique choice to love.

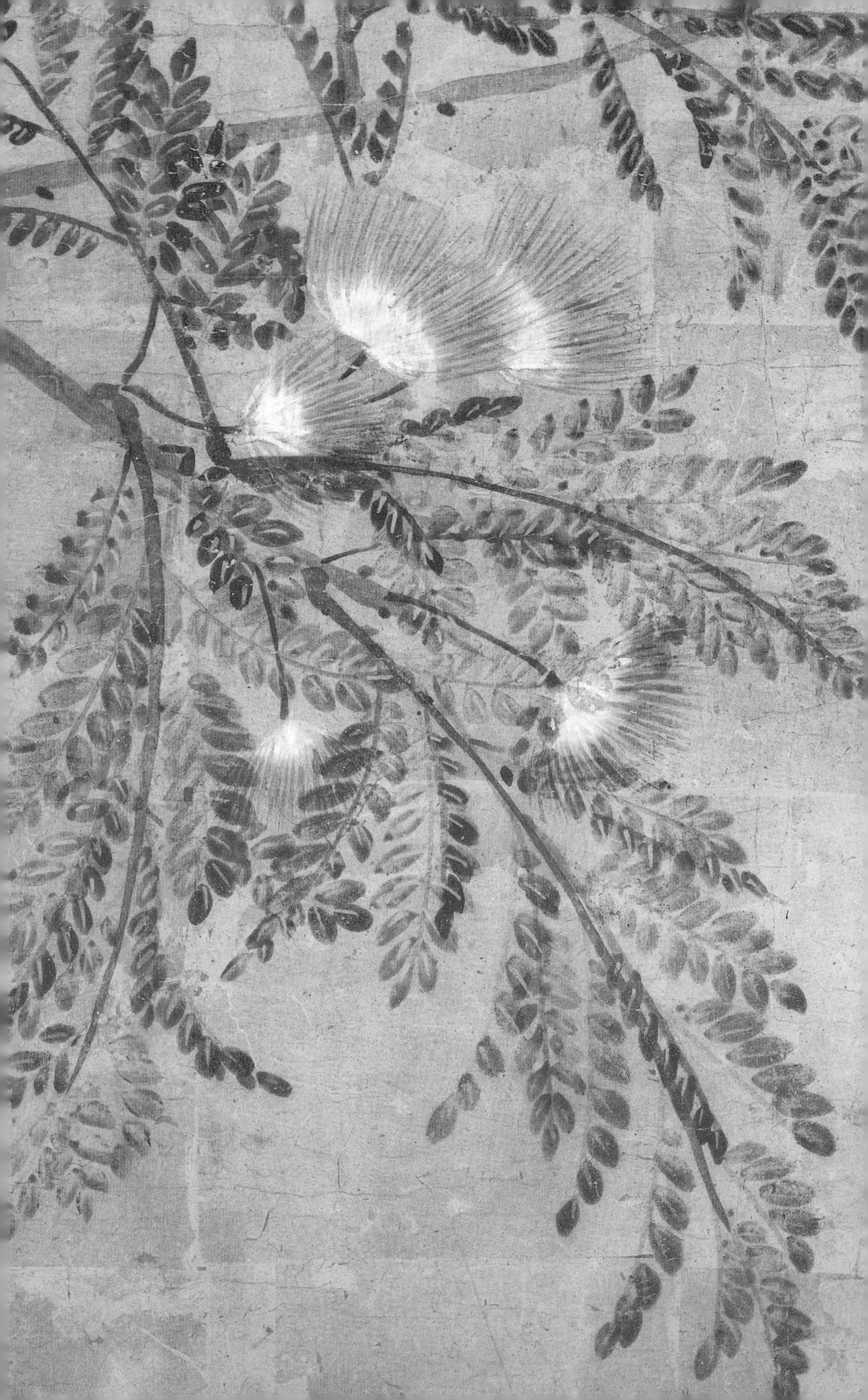

LIGHT OF GRACE

The joy of love is in the stars that
    cloak the earth at night,
And hold the woe of sins at length
    till early morning sight.

The sun reveals the blooms of hope
    that grow with fine intent,
Taking the pain of loss inside
    with pride and faith unbent.

A thousand leaves of hallowed truths
    surround the heart with vines,
To protect the soul from savage deeds
    through fiery battle lines.

The spirit of the world endures
    in heaven's warm embrace,
Defying flames of cruel distress
    to reach the light of grace.

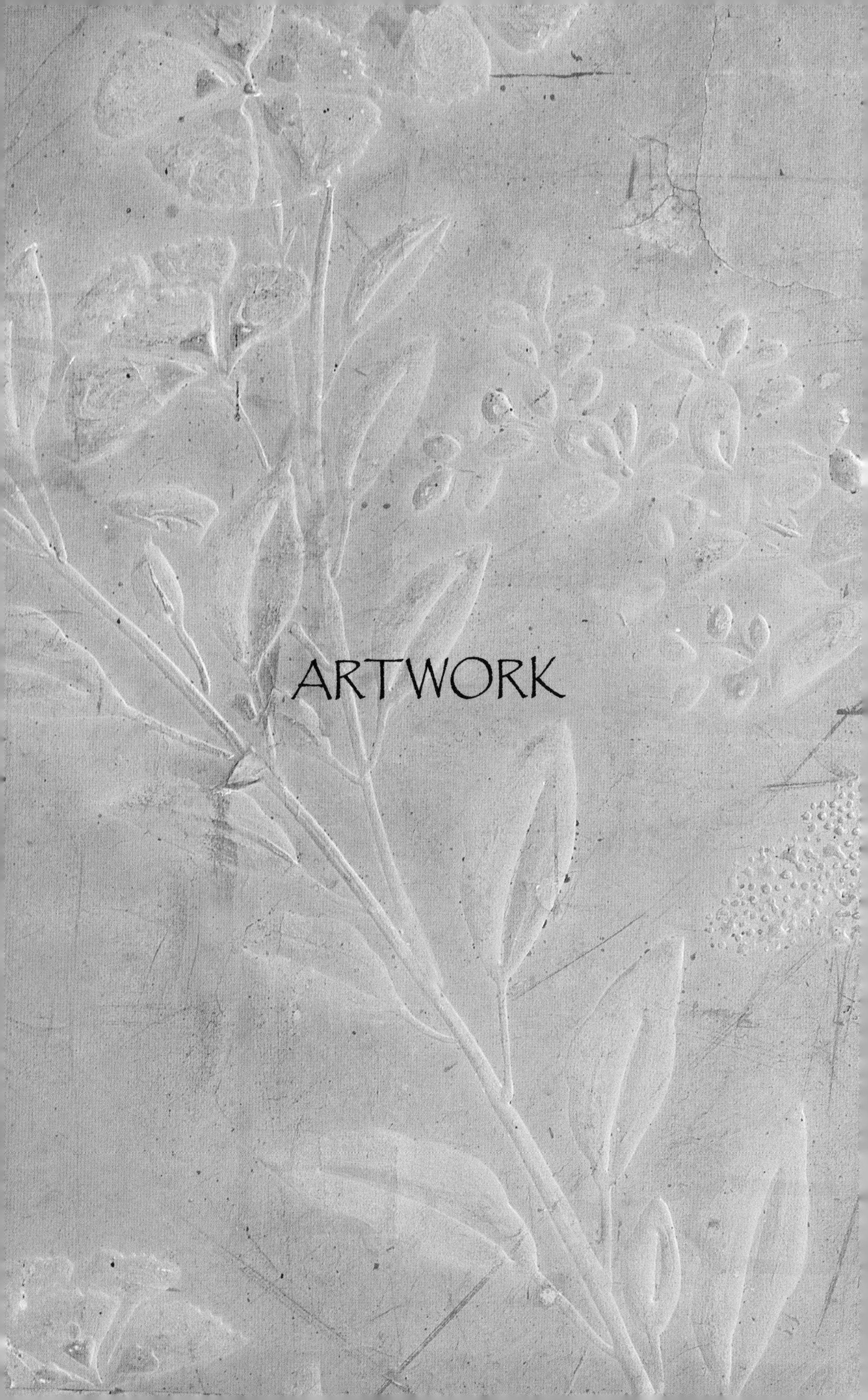

ARTWORK

All artworks are copyright ©
Freer Gallery of Art,
Smithsonian Instituton,
Washington, DC
Gift of Charles Lang Freer

Mimosa tree, poppies, hollyhocks,
and other flowers
Sosetsu, active mid-17th century
Japanese, Edo period, 1630–1670
Four-panel screen: ink, color, and
gold on paper
H×W: 167.4 × 353.4 cm (65 7/8 × 139 1/8 in)
F1902.92

SECTION TITLES

F1902.92 det 2

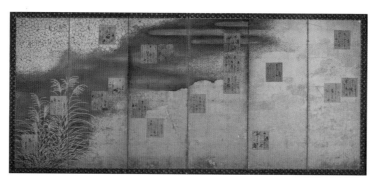

Flowers, grasses, a bamboo blind, and
18 decorated and inscribed poem papers
Hon'ami Koetsu, 1558–1637
Japanese, Edo period, early 17th century
Gold and slight color on paper
H×W: 168.2 × 377.2 cm (66 1/4 × 148 1/2 in)
F1902.196

ARTWORK TITLE

F1902.196 det 5a

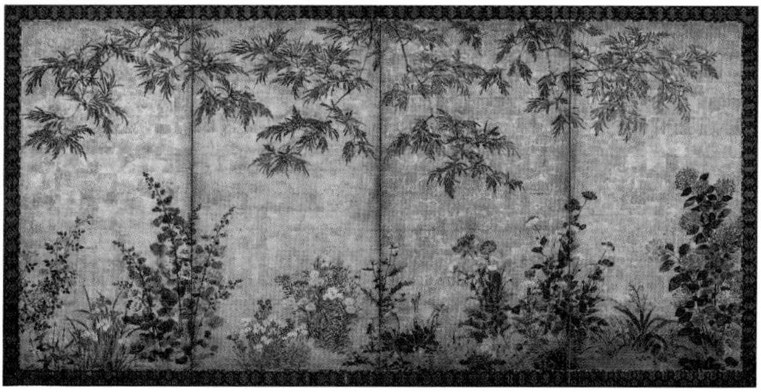

Mimosa tree, poppies, hollyhocks, and other flowers
Sosetsu, active mid-17th century
Japanese, Edo period, 1630-1670
Four-panel screen: ink, color, and gold on paper
HxW: 167.4 × 353.4 cm (65 7/8 × 139 1/8 in)
F1902.92

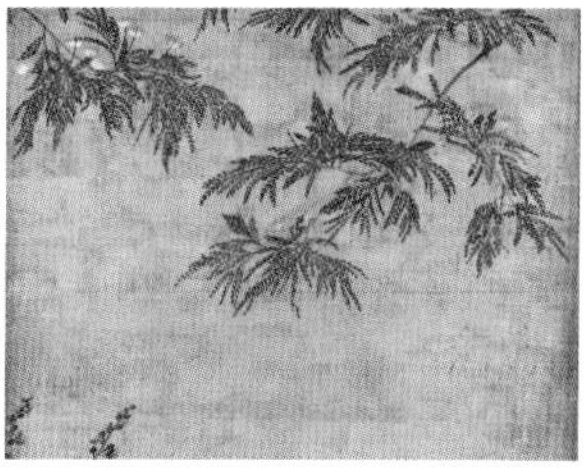

F1902.92 det 3

CELESTIAL DESIGN

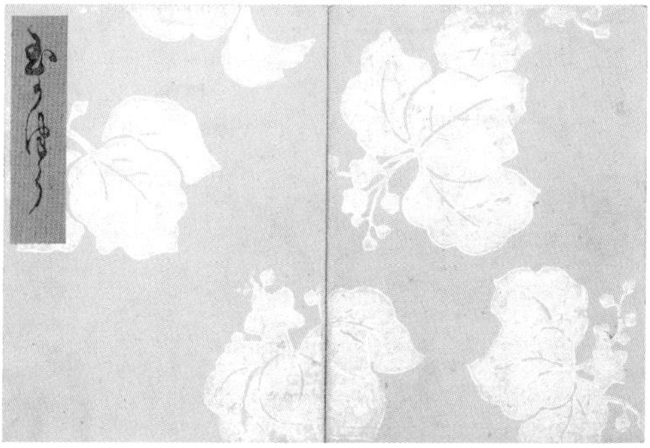

Utaibon, 18-19th centuries,
from the Rare Book Collection,
Freer Gallery of Art,
Arthur M. Sackler Gallery,
Smithsonian Institution Libraries
822-U8-Utaibon20

822-U8-Utaibon20

HEAVENLY ORDER

Summer and autumn flowers
Japanese, Edo period, 1615–1868
Color over gold on paper
H×W (overall): 181 × 377.9 cm
(71 1/4 × 148 3/4 in)
F1896.82

WAR

F1896.82 det 4

Imperial Anthology, Kokinshu
Hon'ami Koetsu, 1558–1637
Tawaraya Sotatsu, fl. ca. 1600–1643
Japan, Momoyama or Edo period, early 17th century
Handscroll: ink, gold, silver, and mica on paper
H×W (overall): 33 × 1021.7 cm (13 × 402 1/4 in)
H×W (decorative panel): 33 × 26.6 cm (13 × 10 1/2 in)
H×W (image): 33 × 968.3 cm (13 × 381 1/4 in)
F1903.309 sec 11
F1903.309 sec 11 det 1

CHILDREN OF PAIN

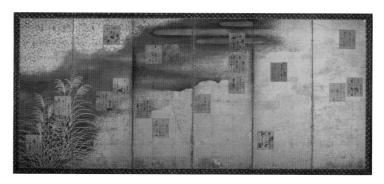

Flowers, grasses, a bamboo blind, and 18
decorated and inscribed poem papers
Hon'ami Koetsu, 1558–1637
Japanese, Edo period, early 17th century
Gold and slight color on paper
H×W: 168.2 × 377.2 cm (66 1/4 × 148 1/5 in)
F1902.196

F1902.196 det 4

KINDNESS OF HEART

Fans and clouds over rocks and water
Hon'ami Koetsu, 1558–1637
Japanese, Edo period, early 17th century
Six-panel folding screen: ink, color, gold,
and silver on paper
H×W: 171.2 × 382.2 cm (67 3/8 × 150 1/2 in)
F1903.121

F1903.121 det 6

WAVES OF HUNGER

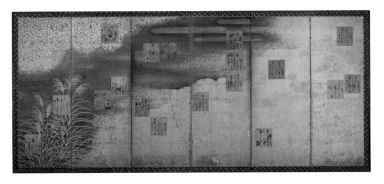

Flowers, grasses, a bamboo blind, and
18 decorated and inscribed poem papers
Hon'ami Koetsu, 1558–1637
Japanese, Edo period, early 17th century
Gold and slight color on paper
H×W: 168.2 × 377.2 cm (66 1/4 × 148 1/5 in)
F1902.196

LEAVES OF HOPE   F1902.196 det 5

Imperial Anthology, Kokinshu
Hon'ami Koetsu, 1558–1637
Tawaraya Sotatsu, fl. ca. 1600–1643
Japan, Momoyama or Edo period, early 17th century
Handscroll: ink, gold, silver, and mica on paper
H×W (overall): 33 × 1021.7 cm (13 × 402 1/4 in)
H×W (decorative panel): 33 × 26.6 cm (13 × 10 1/2 in)
H×W (image): 33 × 968.3 cm (13 × 381 1/4 in)
F1903.309 sec 12

CHAINS OF FEAR   F1903.309 sec 12 det

Mimosa tree, poppies, hollyhocks,
and other flowers
Sosetsu, active mid-17th century
Japanese, Edo period, 1630–1670
Four-panel screen: ink, color, and
gold on paper
H×W: 167.4 × 353.4 cm (65 7/8 × 139 1/8 in)
F1902.92

F1902.92 det 2.2

SPIRIT OF VALOR

Utaibon, 18–19th centuries,
from the Rare Book Collection,
Freer Gallery of Art,
Arthur M. Sackler Gallery,
Smithsonian Institution Libraries
322-U8-Utaibon 08

322-U8-Utaibon 08 det

CLOUDS OF ANGER

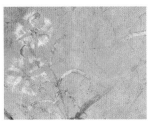

Fans and clouds over rocks and water
Hon'ami Koetsu, 1558–1637
Japanese, Edo period, early 17th century
Six-panel folding screen: ink, color, gold,
and silver on paper
H×W: 171.2 × 382.2 cm (67 3/8 × 150 1/2 in)
F1903.120

PASSION FOR FAIRNESS   F1903.120 det 3

Utaibon, 18–19th centuries,
from the Rare Book Collection,
Freer Gallery of Art,
Arthur M. Sackler Gallery,
Smithsonian Institution Libraries
822-U8-Utaibon 16

SHELTER   822-U8-Utaibon 16 det

Summer and autumn flowers
Japanese, Edo period, 1615–1868
Color over gold on paper
H×W (overall): 181 × 377.9 cm
(71 1/4 × 148 3/4 in)
F1896.82

F1896.82 det 2

A SEA OF TRANQUILITY

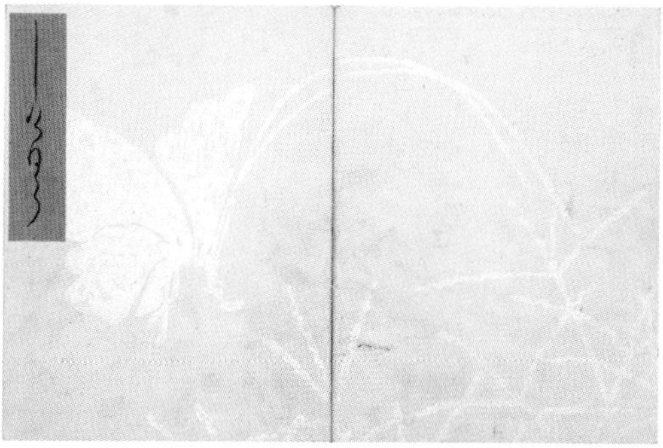

Utaibon, 18–19th centuries,
from the Rare Book Collection,
Freer Gallery of Art,
Arthur M. Sackler Gallery,
Smithsonian Institution Libraries
822-US-Utaibon 02

822-US-Utaibon 02 det

PURSUIT OF RAPTURE

Utaibon, 18–19th centuries,
from the Rare Book Collection,
Freer Gallery of Art,
Arthur M. Sackler Gallery,
Smithsonian Institution Libraries
822-U8-Utaibon 09

PETALS OF JOY

822-U8-Utaibon 09 det

Mimosa tree, poppies, hollyhocks,
and other flowers
Sosetsu, active mid-17th century
Japanese, Edo period, 1630–1670
Four-panel screen: ink, color, and
gold on paper
H×W: 167.4 × 353.4 cm (65 7/8 × 139 1/8 in)
F1902.92

TORN HEART

F1902.92 det 4

Utaibon, 18–19th centuries,
from the Rare Book Collection,
Freer Gallery of Art,
Arthur M. Sackler Gallery,
Smithsonian Institution Libraries
822-US-Utaibon II

822-US-Utaibon II det

FORGIVNESS

Summer and autumn flowers
Japanese, Edo period, 1615–1868
Color over gold on paper
H×W (overall): 181 × 377.9 cm
(71 1/4 × 148 3/4 in)
F1896.82

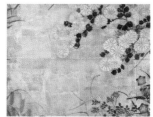

F1896.82 det 4.2

BEYOND EARTH'S RIM

Utaibon, 18-19th centuries,
from the Rare Book Collection,
Freer Gallery of Art,
Arthur M. Sackler Gallery,
Smithsonian Institution Libraries
822-U8-Utaibon 21

MIST OF LOVE

822-U8-Utaibon 21 det

Mimosa tree, poppies, hollyhocks,
and other flowers
Sosetsu, active mid-17th century
Japanese, Edo period, 1630-1670
Four-panel screen: ink, color, and
gold on paper
H×W: 167.4 × 353.4 cm (65 7/8 × 139 1/8 in)
F1902.92

SEARCHING

F1902.92 det 1.2

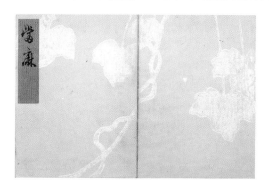

Utaibon, 18–19th centuries,
from the Rare Book Collection,
Freer Gallery of Art,
Arthur M. Sackler Gallery,
Smithsonian Institution Libraries
822-U8-Utaibon 15

822-U8-Utaibon 15 det

KNOTS OF ARROGANCE

Summer and autumn flowers
Japanese, Edo period, 1615–1868
Color over gold on paper
H×W (overall): 181 × 377.9 cm
(71 1/4 × 148 3/4 in)
F1896.82

F1896.82 det 3

RAYS OF COMPASSION

PATH TO WISDOM

Imperial Anthology, Kokinshu
Hon'ami Koetsu, 1558–1637
Tawaraya Sotatsu, fl. ca. 1600–1643
Japan, Momoyama or Edo period, early 17th century
Handscroll: ink, gold, silver, and mica on paper
H×W (overall): 33 × 1021.7 cm (13 × 402 1/4 in)
H×W (decorative panel): 33 × 26.6 cm (13 × 10 1/2 in)
H×W (image): 33 × 968.3 cm (13 × 381 1/4 in)
F1903.309 sec 09
F1903.309 sec 09 det 2

BLOSSOM OF HOPE

Utaibon, 18–19th centuries,
from the Rare Book Collection,
Freer Gallery of Art,
Arthur M. Sackler Gallery,
Smithsonian Institution Libraries
822-U8-Utaibon 12

822-U8-Utaibon 12 det

Mimosa tree, poppies, hollyhocks,
and other flowers
Sosetsu, active mid-17th century
Japanese, Edo period, 1630–1670
Four-panel screen: ink, color, and
gold on paper
H×W: 167.4 × 353.4 cm (65 7/8 × 139 1/8 in)
F1902.92

F1902.92 det 1

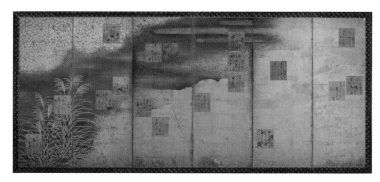

Flowers, grasses, a bamboo blind, and
18 decorated and inscribed poem papers
Hon'ami Koetsu, 1558–1637
Japanese, Edo period, early 17th century
Gold and slight color on paper
H×W: 168.2 × 377.2 cm (66.25 × 148.5 in)
F1902.196

F1902.196 det 3

LIGHT OF GRACE

ENDPAPERS

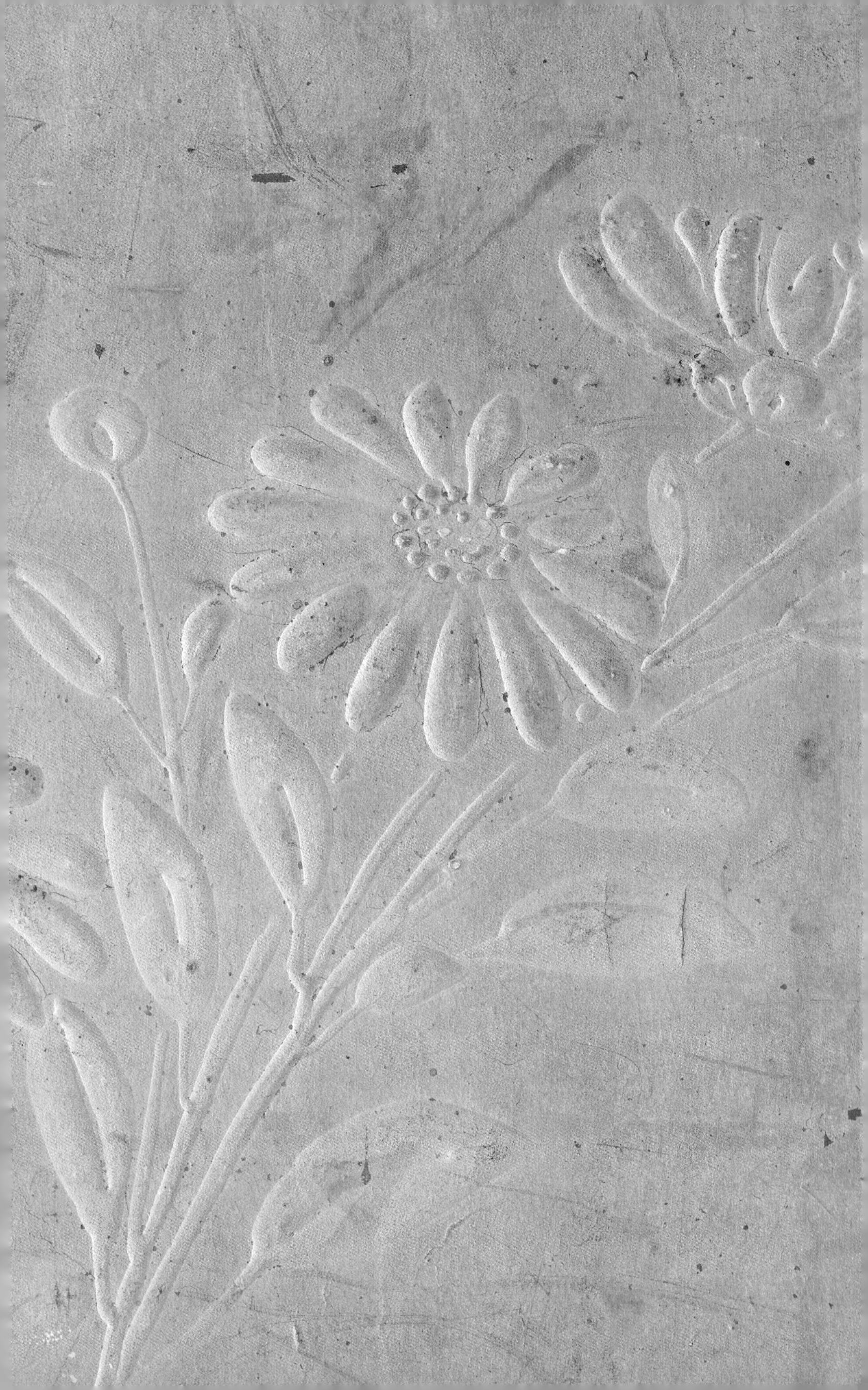

ACKNOWLEDGMENTS

Flowers, grasses, a bambooblind, and
18 decorated and inscribed poem papers
Hon'ami Koetsu, 1558-1637
Japanese, Edo period, early 17th century
Gold and slight color on paper
HxW: 168.2 x 377.2 cm (66 1/4 x 148 1/2 in)
F1902.196 det 3.2

Freer Gallery of Art;
Smithsonian Institution, Washington, D.C.:
Gift of Charles Lang Freer, F 1902.196

Rare and touching images from the past have now inspired me through two books of poetry. *Healing Light* was the result of a prayer after September 11, 2001. *Heavenly Order* has come from a desire to deepen my connection with the creative process of linking my words with beautiful images.

In that regard, I would like first and foremost, to thank Dr. Julian Raby, Director of the Freer Gallery of Art and the Arthur M. Sackler Gallery in Washington D.C., and Dr. James T. Ulak, the Deputy Director, for their considerate and generous assistance in my endeavors. Their unfailing courtesy in listening to my ideas and, in this instance, opening the exquisite Freer collection of Japanese art from the seventeenth to the nineteenth centuries, provided me with a precious sanctuary from which to work.

I would like to extend a particular note of appreciation to the entire staff of the Freer and Sackler Galleries for their invaluable support, most notably, Louise Caldi, Cory Grace, David Hogge, Carol Huh, Kathryn Phillips, Sarah Nolan, Asheley Smith, Ann Yonemura, Reiko Yoshimura, and Katie Ziglar. I reserve special, heartfelt thanks for Neil Greentree for his extraordinary photography.

Warm appreciation goes to Dr. Felice Fischer, Curator of Japanese and East Asian Art at the Philadelphia Museum of Art, and Holly Frisbee of the Rights and Reproductions department for their kind assistance.

My deepest thanks go to my gifted publisher, Marta Hallett, and her team at Glitterati Incorporated, including Gayatri Mullapudi, for once again believing in my efforts. I would also like to thank Bruce Sanford for his fine literary counsel. I am especially appreciative of the talented technical assistance I had from Marta Lapinska and Henrique Siblesz, as well as from Antonio Alcalá and Sarah Magee, in implementing my vision of Heavenly Order.

No words can adequately express my loving gratitude to Arnaud, my beloved husband of almost forty years, for inspiring me everyday with his wisdom, courage, and strength, and for not complaining once about my long hours away from him. I thank, too, my dear brother, Dimitri Villard, and my sister-in-law Xue Er, for their cherished loyalty.

The beauty of Japanese art has entranced me, and I am most grateful to His Excellency Ryozo Kato, the Ambassador of Japan, and Mrs. Kato for their kind interest in the book and their gracious hospitality.

In August of 2004, my erudite friend of many years, Grega Daly, sent me an inspirational book, OFFERINGS, about Buddhist wisdom, and her distinguished husband, Leo Daly, invited me to join the Advisory Council of the Asia Society. I treasured their thoughtful gestures at the time and I thank them with my heart.

I could not have written this book without the patient ear and wise counsel of my unique friend, Isabel Jasinowski, whose caring daily calls encouraged me to go further in my quest each time we spoke.

Fond thanks go to Frank Andrews, for his amazing insight; Laurel Colless, for her sympathetic support; Roland Flamini, for casting his fine eye on my work; and Diane Flamini, for her gentle patience; Lorna Graev, for warmly offering her lifelong friendship and lovely home to me; Hillie Mahoney, for sharing her extensive knowledge of Japan and giving me her brilliant perspective; Ann Nitze, for generously searching her library and lending me her stunning books on Japanese art from the Edo period; Lucky Roosevelt, for bringing her fabulous experience of life to reading the first poems I wrote for the book; Michael Sonnenreich, for his many superb suggestions concerning the choice of art; and Katherine Wood, for her unwavering encouragement.

Thank you to the dear ones who have kindly helped in one way or another with *Heavenly Order*. I simply could not have dedicated my time to completing this book without Stanley Stefan's devoted and generous efforts and Sonia Wallace's faithful assistance.

I know there are many others who have given me so much kindness and support and I thank them here with all my love.

We are engaged in an increasingly difficult world where challenges from dark forces test our courage and strength. And yet I am thankful each day to my parents for bringing me to this earth and teaching me the joy of love and kindness.

Lucien Capehart

Alexandra Villard de Borchgrave has built a reputation as a photojournalist, author, and poet. Her photographs have appeared on the covers of internationally renowned publications, such as *Newsweek* and *Paris Match*. She is the co-author of *Villard: The Life and Times of an American Titan* (Nan A. Talese/Doubleday), a biography of her great grandfather, railroad magnate and financier Henry Villard, who masterminded the creation of General Electric. She is also the author of *Healing Light: Thirty Messages of Love, Hope, and Courage* (Glitterati Incorporated). She currently serves on the Board of the Blair House Restoration Fund and the Advisory Committee of the Asia Society. She is a graduate of Sarah Lawrence College and lives with her husband in Washington, D.C.